THE FULL CONTACT RULES FOR BUSINESS

*How to Not
Screw Up Your
Business in the Era
of Globalization*

BRIAN KEITH JONES

Outskirts Press, Inc.
Denver, Colorado

The Full Contact Rules for Business
How to Not Screw Up Your Business in the Era of Globalization
All Rights Reserved
Copyright © 2007 Brian Keith Jones
V3.0

Outskirts Press
http://www.outskirtspress.com

ISBN-13: 978-1-4327-0806-1

Library of Congress Control Number: 2007928617

Contents

Introduction
The Opening Kickoff

Allow me to initiate this journey with the obligatory academic introduction to any book attempting to legitimize the virtues of managing a business. Leading any modern organization is one of the most challenging professions that anyone can choose to pursue as a vocation. The rapidly evolving landscape of the global economy virtually guarantees that the complexity of business analysis, and the speed with which decisions must be made and implemented, will demand an increasingly high level of sophistication in the future. The challenges ahead will undoubtedly demand a mixture of formal educational tools, experience across a variety of disciplines, and the surprisingly rare ability to make timely decisions. The best leaders have always possessed these abilities; however, increasingly, they not only must have the ability to implement strategies, but also the willingness to continually adapt them as conditions shift in unexpected directions. It is the recognition that it's increasingly foolish to cling to a vision, even as changes make the most meticulous of plans irrelevant, that separates the great leaders from those who perpetually underachieve regardless of their resume.

Your formal education is impressive. Your business knowledge is well rounded and encompasses a variety of disciplines. Your ability to communicate concepts and plans is universally acknowledged by your peers. In short, you have accumulated all of the abilities essential for leading the discussion at the next company retreat. These accomplishments may even result in you landing that key promotion that you have worked so diligently to achieve. Unfortunately, it's time for reality to make an appearance.

Professional football quarterbacks all possess the ability to break down the details and objectives of every play, and then intelligently dissect them to make the necessary adjustments while in the comfortable confines of the film room. However, the only thing that actually matters is what decisions he makes on third and eleven, the team down by five points, less than two minutes remaining on the clock, and an all-pro linebacker closing in from the back side. How does he respond when he is actually facing the pressures of game conditions? Philosophically knowing how to play the game makes for insightful discussions, but successfully playing the game is the only way to win.

All of this higher intellect acknowledged, this book has nothing to do with the recognized science of management. After over twenty years of life in corporate America, I was unexpectedly presented with the opportunity to do what most managers in business claim that they would like to do — I became a business owner. Up to that moment of my career, I had followed the timeworn checklist prescribed for the successful corporate manager:

> ➢ Attended college and earned the prerequisite undergraduate degree.
> ➢ Accepted an entry-level position at a company that offered a promising career path.
> ➢ Worked the overtime and took on the extra projects to improve my position.
> ➢ Uprooted my young family twice to broaden my experience and exposure.
> ➢ Committed to the all-consuming, and ridiculous, schedule that allowed me to finish my graduate degree at night while raising three kids.
> ➢ Became involved in acquisitions and divestitures.
> ➢ Was promoted to the corporate staff level.
> ➢ Made countless presentations regarding past results, and detailed yearly plans mapping out the future direction of the company.
> ➢ Spent years on airplanes and in hotel rooms, traveling to operations and meeting with customers and suppliers around the world.
> ➢ Left the corporate life for my own company.

> ➤ Ran headfirst into reality, and suddenly realized just how little I knew about actually running a successful business.

Almost immediately, it became obvious that if I insisted on managing based on my so-called world-class education and experience, my dream company would wither away, and there would be no escaping that it was my fault. It quickly became a race; could I shed all of the corporate garbage that had somehow seemed so essential to "proper" management a few months earlier, and rediscover reality, enabling me to begin to focus on those things that actually mattered in making the business successful? The watershed moment in the history of the company was when it became apparent even to me that my years of education and corporate experience had smothered my common sense, and my new adventure was going to relentlessly demand that I learn the real fundamentals of running a business.

Once I had taken that painful first step, confessed my sorry state, and come to terms with the reality that my brilliant career amounted to little more than the needless sacrifice of countless trees to produce nonsensical plans and overly detailed summaries, neither of which anyone bothered to read, could I move forward. My new management group held their collective breaths, unplugged the "essential" MRP system, tossed the work instructions in the garbage, and eliminated any positions where I couldn't even understand the job description. I then jumped in headfirst and began the painful exercise of actually learning the intricacies of the business I had just invested my life into. Over the next six months I managed to clear away much of the smoke from the organization, divorced myself from all of the common knowledge I had once held so dear, and learned more about managing a business in that short span than in the previous twenty years. Humbled, but wiser, the company began to turn the corner and made rapid strides forward, well beyond what any of us could have hoped for based on past experience.

With that historical lesson established, the objective of this project is to address those essential elements that formal education has long since left behind, and the corporate world has replaced with programs and philosophies peddled by those who have confused management with an overly self-righteous sermon. The task is to help protect you from becoming so entangled in the chaos of the typical working day in our increasingly frantic world that you don't do something stupid. Or, more likely, overlook the obvious, and in turn, do lasting damage to your business. More times than not, it's not the strategic or analytical blunders that doom organizations to failure, but the small, seemingly obvious oversights that lead to frustratingly poor results, or even failure. In truth, they aren't small parts of your business, just ordinary. At its foundation, the objective of this book is to encourage you to continually take a step back and ask the question, "Can anyone explain why are we doing this?"

There are business schools and programs of varying quality across the country, indeed, throughout the world. There are seminars, online classes, books, and lectures, all offering their versions of a formal business education. Despite all of this access to knowledge, you can have all of the talent, degrees, certifications, and experience in the world, and yet still fail because, in Biblical terms, you have built your house on sand. You become a victim of that basic lack of common sense that has somehow been squeezed out of most companies. They are the "death by a thousand pinpricks" issues that have caused even the most sophisticated organizations to falter. At the most basic level, they are the timeless realities that my kids affectionately describe to me as "No duh."

The game plans of professional football teams are thoroughly researched and analyzed, then painstakingly developed. Every detail is planned out, each assignment drilled and reinforced. Strengths and weaknesses aren't a secret, the weather is the same for both teams, and plans can be adjusted as the game unfolds. However, even with all of this preparation and commitment to excellence, invariably, it is the illegal motion at an inopportune time, a bad exchange between quarterback and center that results in a fumble, or a missed block that leads to a sack and takes the team out of field goal range that ultimately determines who wins, and who loses. It's the small things, the neglect of basic fundamentals that get in the way of executing the plan and winning the game.

Unfortunately, in the business world, not only are common sense mistakes made with frightening frequency, they are often ignored, and as a result, destined to repeat themselves until the organization eventually implodes. Many times, the more trouble a company gets into by neglecting these seemingly small issues, the more sophisticated their rescue plans become, resulting in even less focus on the fundamentals. Company-wide reorganizations are then initiated because they have to do something, and invariably, lead to their only possible conclusion — the next reorganization. These basics are essential to your business because they represent the very foundation that you put all of your education and experience on. The mystery remains — why are they ignored and overlooked with such regularity?

- ➢ Managers make the fatal mistake of assuming that these fundamentals are being followed.
- ➢ They are consumed with the increasingly complex issues associated with running a modern business, and allow themselves to become disconnected from the details. As a result:
  - o They become immersed in the company issues of the moment, preparing for the next reporting cycle, or reporting results concerning the last reporting cycle in a manner to make them appear better than they actually were.
  - o They neglect to acknowledge that everything they do, everything that the business does, must have a positive impact on the value of the organization. If not, it's nothing more than wasted energy.
- ➢ Management frequently confuses doing it ***their*** way, or the way that corporate policy dictates, with doing it the ***right*** way.
- ➢ Management and academia have become so caught up in enlightening everyone regarding their next great insight that they neglect reinforcing common sense.

No coach was ever acknowledged as being revolutionary because he pointed out that his running back's shoelaces were untied. Nevertheless, it's essential that it be corrected. If the back trips over his laces behind the line of scrimmage, all of the training, all the time in the weight room, all of the practice and time designing the play, were irrelevant.

More likely, a more honest explanation is that the basics are overlooked with such regularity because they are oftentimes the boring, painful aspects of running an organization, and many managers prefer not to deal with them. They are either uncomfortable to address, or just not very exciting. Managers gravitate toward areas that are more stimulating or they are more comfortable with, leaving hope to manage the more mundane details.

As I will come back to time and time again, your business is the details. More precisely, the small details found quietly hiding within the foundation of your organization. My objective here isn't to be overly complex or uniquely insightful, but simply to provide you with issues to consider. In a world where we tend to overcomplicate everything, I will err on the side of oversimplification. I will try and make you, and your organization, better because you took the time to read this material. If not, this exercise is simply a waste of time, both yours and mine. This represents an investment, and like any investment, it must have a return.

What I am not trying to do is make you feel good about your management abilities, personal talents, leadership or even your intellect. The more that I can make you uneasy about what you are doing, the better I feel about it. I want to challenge you, make you think, make you angry, and if possible, even offend you from time to time. I will criticize the way you go about your business, and, through the use of football analogies, even imply that some of the things you hold so dear are actually nothing short of stupid. Of the twenty areas addressed, if you come away thinking that nineteen of them are useless, but one challenges your current thinking, I will have satisfied my objective. My commitment is to making you uncomfortable, and keeping you that way. The feel-good management theories of the day that promise to make your life easier won't be found in these pages.

Sorry, but I just don't care. That mind-set may have its place, but not here. No nice, polite management techniques to make you feel better about your deteriorating bottom line or accelerating global competition. There are plenty of those philosophies being offered up, and countless high-priced consultants that can be brought in, or non-productive executives internally that can be promoted, to enlighten you. You are participating in an increasingly hard fought contest, and I would strongly recommend that you reconsider all insights that suggest winning comes with a minimal cost.

In the business world of today you should never be too comfortable, and if you are, chances are you are in denial. Things are moving fast, and

6

you can't afford to trip over the details because you were too busy, or feeling too good about yourself. I want to not only help you to create a sense of urgency in your organization; I want you to create a permanent state of controlled urgency. I want it to become a way of life for your business, because that is the only way that you are going to remain consistently successful in the future.

Let's start with the format utilized for the material throughout this presentation. Each chapter is presented in outline form to provide the information, and nothing else. As impressive as it might be, you don't need to see all of the ways that I can use an adjective. I was once given some advice that has proven time and time again to be profound: "Write what matters, say what is needed. Write only what matters, say only what is needed."

- ➢ I will get to each point of emphasis and move on, making it simple to re-access any areas of particular interest and leave space for your thoughts.
  - o I will bring up the issues and make it uncomfortable for you not to deal with them.
- ➢ In keeping with the minimalist spirit, all chapters were written with the objective — the shorter, the better.
  - o I want to encourage you to consider or discuss the issues, not spend hours reading my insightful analysis.
- ➢ I will never assume that I know how to run your business.
  - o You spend all day, every day, in your profession. I will assume that you know more about your business than I do.
    - ▪ If not, this book, or for that matter any book, isn't going to help; your business is in trouble.
- ➢ I will deal only with the fundamental issues.
  - o Details that you might have overlooked.
  - o Philosophies that you might have taken for granted.
  - o Actions that will cause you to fail if you don't recognize and address them.
  - o Most commonly, things that you inherently are aware of at some level, but have become smothered beneath the piles of corporate mandates being senselessly rained down from above within many businesses.

- Every organization has some hidden rocks lurking dangerously just below the surface; it's just a matter of whether or not they are acknowledged and acted upon.
- ➤ The premise utilized throughout the text is that everyone is a manager.
  - o You may be responsible for an entire corporation, a department, or possibly just the work piling in your cubicle. Regardless, you are managing; that is how you will be treated and how you should act.

Why the use of football analogies? How to best capture these overlooked, seemingly mundane organizational and behavioral flaws became one of my most cumbersome challenges in trying to emphasize how critical they are within a company. More specifically, how dangerous they can be within a business if neglected. One Sunday afternoon, while watching a football game, it occurred to me that fans are extremely intolerant of sloppy execution, mistakes due to poor preparation, lack of effort, and an endless list of other shortcomings that are debated after nearly every play. However, for some unexplainable reason, these same people seemed to consider similar behavior in their own professional lives as annoying realities to be tolerated. At that moment, the game of football became the acid test for evaluating rationality. Take the annoying self-destructive tendencies found within any organization, and then check their sanity on the football field. By comparing the office to the gridiron, there are three basic objectives:

1. *Hopefully, I can break away from prototypical business writing, which has developed into one of the most boring instructional genres ever created, and make it more interesting. Business is incredibly fast moving, and the pace is exploding. However, the typical business book plods along at such a lethargic pace that by the time you reach the end, the world has changed, and the information is irrelevant.*
2. *By taking the things that happen around the office on a daily basis and then placing them in a completely foreign environment, we can begin to consider if what you are doing*

actually makes sense. Once issues are exposed as being counterproductive, or even destructive, it will become impossible not to address them without being irresponsible.

3. *Let's face it; it's just more fun — particularly for me. If you think reading a business book can get boring, try writing one.*

Additionally, fundamentally, football is the sport that consistently mirrors the business world. Player on player, competing at the most basic human level; yet simultaneously, the most complex of all games, with comprehensive game plans and specific position assignments that are all interdependent. The playbook may be several hundred pages long, but a single detail at the bottom of page sixty-seven is critical to the execution of the game plan. It's essential that the team has an overall strategy, or they will fail. Players must to be continually developed and challenged to reach their potential. One player cannot carry the whole team, regardless of what they believe; everyone must work together. The team must always keep improving or they will find themselves taking a beating on a weekly basis. The situation on the field keeps changing, and if they fail to constantly adapt, they will lose.

Players change, coaches change, unexpected competition pops up, or weather conditions demand that they scrap plans in the middle of the game. Every player has their own unique assignments, training and talents; however, if they don't coordinate their efforts toward a common goal, they will fail. And in the end, the coach gets the credit when the teams wins, the blame when it loses. Their customers may appreciate all of the team's past efforts, but what they are really interested in is how the team performs in the next game.

Another benefit is that professional football is a hard, cold business, and although we all have to manage our way through life, dealing with the real issues of real people, managers must possess the ability to see things as they actually are. The focus mandated in assembling and maintaining a winning football franchise demands that teams constantly face reality, whether they like it or not. While it may be accurate that you are managing a business rather than playing a football game, it demands consideration that if a situation makes no sense for a team, possibly it doesn't make sense in your profession, either. By placing decisions and routines into the basic structure of a football team, some of the things you do will not only stop making sense, they will seem outrageous. If nothing else, it provides a new and unique reference point, which is always worthy of consideration.

Although through the years I have seen an endless variety of creative ways to screw up an organization, in the end, I selected the twenty stumbling blocks that I keep running across time and again. They make their appearance regardless of whether the business I may be working with is large or small, manufacturing or service based. Each chapter will deal with one of these all too common company killers.

It's the quarterback who loses his discipline and can't resist throwing the ball back across his body and into double coverage, even though every coach since grade school repeatedly taught him otherwise. It's the cornerback who bites on a play action fake while in single coverage on third and eleven, and surrenders a crucial touchdown late in the game. It's the noseguard that lines up in the neutral zone on fourth and one, giving the opponent a free first down.

These are the issues that many managers just never seem to learn, and although you may find that many examples don't apply to your situation, the reality is, when most professionals are honest, many hit much closer to home than they are comfortable with. The truth be told, not only have most managers struggled with these basic fundamentals at some point in their careers, many continue to repeat these mistakes on a regular basis.

So, put away your presuppositions on how to manage a company and put on your helmet and pads. Let's see how your organization, and your management style, stacks up in the full-contact world of modern business.

Chapter **1**

Training Camp
Back to the Basics

In the world of professional football, the opening of training camp represents that dreaded start to every season where the coaching staff begins the process of reinforcing the fundamentals and disciplines that will ultimately determine much of the success of the upcoming season. The players are relentlessly drilled on the intricacies of their positions in an effort to make their reactions to game situations second nature during the heat of the battle. Regardless of how many years the player has played the game, or been with the team, it is a time when everyone has to endure long practices, meetings, film analysis, and then more practice to reinforce the basics of the game. Through blood and sweat, the coaching staff pounds away at the same fundamentals that are taught to grade school kids before they take the field for their first flag football game. No detail is considered too small to practice until it is burned into the player's psyche. No one looks forward to it; however, in the ultra-competitive world of professional football, where the separation between teams is increasingly narrow, it is an essential, and unavoidable, part of the game.

The offensive coordinator obsesses with getting a clean exchange between the quarterback and the running back on every play. It may be the most taken for granted part of the game, yet if not done correctly, the relevancy of the play called, the hours of time spent perfecting execution, and the efforts of the other players on the field are meaningless. The defensive coordinator examines the spacing along the line, blowing drills dead and correcting players at even the slightest misalignment. Every defensive set relies on each player maintaining a strict discipline. The special teams coach explains over and over the precise angle that each player must maintain on kickoff coverage, repeatedly reminding everyone on the field that this might be their only opportunity to make the team, and he cannot afford to keep a player who doesn't get it right every time. The complexities of each offensive and defensive set will be rapidly introduced throughout camp; however, it is these basic fundamentals of the game that the coaches know will ultimately determine the outcome each week, and they are uncompromising in their insistence on proper execution.

- *These essential fundamentals represent the list of keys that the player __must__ do, and they are reminded of such at every opportunity.*
- *At the other extreme are the flaws that __must not__ be done, and likewise, the players are reminded of such at every opportunity.*

➢ Like a coaching staff, there are areas in business that management must constantly reinforce if the organization is going to be consistently successful.
  o My promise is that I will take advantage of every opportunity to pound away at these fundamentals throughout the text.
    ▪ I will be satisfied that I have achieved my objective only when you cringe at the mere sight of them due to their repetition.
➢ In the same manner as our football team, I have separated the positive from the negative:
  o **KEY** fundamentals that ___must___ be done within every organization.
  o **FLAWS** that your company ___must not___ have.
    ▪ I will emphasize these **KEY** points and **FLAWS** in

oversized, bold italics at every possible opportunity.
- I will make an effort to beat them into your mind-set by reinforcing them as if I were blowing a whistle in your ear to constantly repeat a fundamental until it becomes second nature.

➢ Because businesses continually invent new and increasingly creative ways to screw themselves up, developing a list of fundamental **KEYS** and **FLAWS** that covers the issues consistently buried under the weight of corporate activities would appear to be an insurmountable challenge. Regrettably, it was actually quite simple. Regardless of the type or complexity of the business that I have worked with, five **KEY** points, and five **FLAWS** highlight their importance with predictable regularity.
- o The issues where management is insulted that I dared to raise them due to their obvious commitment.
  - Substantive evidence of their support is always much harder to find than their verbal insistence.
- o They are compromised on a daily basis, and only those at the top of the organization are blissfully unaware.
- o They represent the ground-floor fundamentals that your organization simply cannot ignore if you want to succeed the increasingly ultra-competitive world unfolding all around you.

1 - KEY - Business 101

➢ Your business must make a profit, and you must do it in a responsible manner, no exceptions. Businesses must do this to succeed, so why does it seem to be constantly ignored as companies go about their day?
- o It receives consistent lip service; however, in many companies I have a difficult time finding managers who can actually explain specifically how their business makes a profit, and even more disconcerting, how they contribute to that profit.

2 - KEY – Be a professional

➤ This can easily be turned into a long list of characteristics, but it always starts with:
   o Take responsibility for your actions.
      ▪ I find far more managers adept at avoiding responsibility, rather than assuming it.
   o Do what is in the best interest of the organization.
   o Treat people honestly and fairly.
      ▪ This starts with taking ownership of the words that come out of your mouth.
   o Deal with difficult situations as they arise.
   o Always be preparing for what's next.

3 - KEY – Keep asking, Does this make sense?

➤ This single question will keep you from taking actions that not only aren't in the best interest of your company, but also are ridiculous.
   o Never implement a new program or process without taking the time to ask this one question.
   o Take the time to ask this question about everything that you are currently doing.
      ▪ Note: "Because we always do it this way" is not a real answer; it's a cop-out.

4 - KEY – Never get too comfortable

➤ If you are comfortable, you are either in denial or completely out of touch. If your company has not been impacted by globalization, it will be.

- o Most significantly, if your organization doesn't have a sense of urgency, find a way to create one.

5 - KEY – Facts are stubborn things

➤ One of my favorite sayings originated with our second president, John Adams: In the end, you must deal with the facts. An organization cannot ignore or manipulate the facts and be successful. Once you do that, they are no longer the facts, and you cannot make good decisions without being lucky.

- o Facts are the basis of nearly all business decisions; know the facts and deal with them.

These are the <u>must</u> fundamental keys that every player must be consistently capable of executing if the coaching staff is going to keep him on the roster.

- *If a running back wants to play, he <u>must</u> be able to consistently pick up the blitz. If he's not capable, the number of situations where he can be on the field will be severely limited, and could even result in his release from the team.*
- *Defensive players <u>must</u> wrap up the ball carrier. The defensive call was perfect for the offensive play, and every position maintained their assignment perfectly, but if the player in the hole failed to wrap up the ball carrier and make the tackle, the scheme and the assignments mean nothing.*
- *The kickoff team members <u>must</u> stay in their lanes. The loss of discipline of a single player can not only result in a big play for the opponent, but also change the momentum for the entire game.*

1 - Flaw – Bad management

➢ This all too common flaw manifests itself in seemingly endless variations, but I find that the majority of bad managers ultimately can be classified into one of three areas:
  o Weak management — managers that avoid the tough issues and consistently fail to make decisions. On any given day, they tend to waffle between being lazy and fearful.
  o Arrogant management — managers that are too smart to learn what actually needs to be done. They insist on telling others how to fix their areas of responsibility, because they can't manage their own. There is no point in utilizing the potential of those around them, because they already know it all. On most occasions, they make decisions despite the talent around them.
  o Incompetent management — managers that are not up to the task at hand. Consistently poor results can't help but expose these managers; however, for some reason, many survive unchallenged by those above them.
    ▪ This particular flaw permeates so many organizations that I had to fight the urge to include it on every page. Regardless, I did manage to bring it up enough to be irritating.

2 - Flaw – Debating if change is good or bad

➢ A completely ridiculous discussion that consumes many organizations. Management's efforts must be directed toward what actions are required to deal with the changes.
  o Whether or not anyone likes the changes that all businesses face should never be a consideration, and discussing them is a waste of one of your most critical resources: time.

3 - Flaw – Management by fuzzy feeling

➤ This is where you will find the next new program, philosophy, or clever saying. These managers try to drive the business forward with words and new programs, rather than actions based on analysis that lead to measurable results.
   o If you are going to succeed, you must get out of the "feel-good" business.

4 - Flaw – Lack of integrity

➤ Individual careers and lives are destroyed by a lack of integrity. Organizations are destroyed by a lack of integrity. At their foundation, capitalism and free markets are built upon the assumption of integrity.
   o You must be fair.
   o You must be honest.
      ▪ Integrity is an absolute that cannot be compromised.

5 - Flaw – Ask how hard something is

➤ Don't ask if something is hard; ask if it's best. In many businesses, I find that a culture has been created where what is best isn't the primary consideration. The amount of effort and pain involved drives the decisions. This is the natural outflow of management trying to avoid the difficult or challenging issues that are inevitable within every organization.
   o Determine what objectives are essential and then find ways to address them.

*These **must not** mistakes are flaws that have to be eliminated if the* *coaching staff is going to trust the player on the field. Committing these mistakes during training camp is a good way for a player to find himself looking for another line of work.*

- *The offense **must not** turn the ball over. Talent and planning become irrelevant when the quarterback makes an ill-advised pass that leads to an interception, or the running back fails to secure the ball and fumbles.*
- *The defense **must not** lose containment. Players cannot get caught up in trying to make an individual play and compromise the design of the defense and expose the team to big play.*
- *For everyone on the team, they **must not** commit penalties. Offensive penalties kill our team's drive. Defensive penalties keep the opponent's drive alive.*
  - *Yards are battled over with too much effort and pain to give them away for free.*

- ➢ These are the fundament **KEYS** and **FLAWS** that I cannot escape as I work with companies. No matter how much the world changes, these issues remain the same. They are at the core of the majority of struggles I encounter, and although they would seem obvious, many times they are perilously neglected within organizations. They are the details that need to be constantly reinforced if your company is going to be successful.

Consistently performing the basic fundamentals play after play throughout the game will rarely be appreciated by anyone but the coaching staff. Regardless, if they are poorly executed, they will receive a lot of attention from every analyst and armchair coach the next morning. Turnovers, penalties, missed assignments — the "screw-ups" during a game that turn a dominant statistical performance into another loss. They are the mental breakdowns that drive every coach crazy, and send the fans to exits early in the fourth quarter. The game starts with blocking, tackling, and eliminating turnovers. Do these things well, and your team has an excellent foundation for winning games. Neglect them as you implement your brilliant new offensive or defensive scheme, and the losses will pile up.

Chapter 2

First Down
Focus on the Objective

T he primary objective of every business is all too frequently brushed off to the side to accumulate dust while everyone frantically works on the "stuff" of the day that is bearing down all around them. Overall company objectives that often seem distant and unrelated are quickly broken down by management into action items to fulfill job descriptions, which are then tied to improvement plans to meet department goals, which ultimately become monthly targets created in conjunction with a budget imposed by a mystery department. This results in the ultimate goal of the company becoming buried in the noise of the day as everyone races through the corporate maze without the energy to even care about where they are actually headed. The objective of the individual employee becomes nothing more than trying to survive the day. What they create is an organization that has replaced _the_ objective with an endless list of seemingly isolated tasks, and then rewards those that can either do the most "stuff," or convince those above them how much "stuff" they can do. Speed and volume are allowed to trump substance and direction. As a manager, you must take a step back and refocus. Make sure that all of the "stuff" that you are doing, and demanding others do, all leads toward _the_ objective.

➢ Your company has to make money.
  o It is ___the___ starting and ending point for any business. Without it, it's a mathematical certainty that your organization will eventually cease to exist.

KEY - Business 101

  o It is so central to what you are doing that it merits being both a key point and a chapter.
➢ The next objective:
  o Your company has to make money.
    ▪ It's the most succinct possible lesson that I can offer you. If you have any ambition to be successful in business, make sure that you keep this unavoidable fact anchored at the center of your focus and efforts.

Producing a profit in your business is analogous to winning on the football field. There is a good argument for winning being secondary in sports, but not at the professional level. I would be quick to advocate that it is imperative for your local high school coach to put teaching character ahead of wins and losses. If they don't, then the coach is simply living through your kids for his or her own selfish motives and should be immediately replaced.

Flaw – Lack of integrity

Now that my philosophical position relative to youth sports has been established, it's time to grow up. You aren't in high school anymore, and should not be allowed to act as if you are. You are an adult striving to make a living at your chosen profession. You are personally responsible for bringing integrity and character to the job every day. This book clearly demands that you are a professional and should behave as such. After all, you are being paid for what you do. You and your company must win.

KEY – Be a professional

➢ I am always stunned by how many people in business have such a hard time focusing on profitability, or worse yet, choose to ignore that it is essential.
  o Many managers consistently neglect reality for the worst, yet most common of reasons:
    ▪ Making money is hard work, and is becoming progressively more difficult. However, that doesn't make it any less essential.

The team's quarterback is sacked from behind late in the game, quickly jumps up and calls a time-out, and then joins his coach on the sideline.

Quarterback: "Coach, their corners are playing too soft to get the ball deep. We still have two time-outs left, and I need to complete a couple of quick out routes to try and get them to move up. One step in tighter and I'll have a window to throw the ball downfield."

Head Coach: "I've noticed that, too, but I'm concerned about the beating you're taking, and let's face it, mathematically the odds of us pulling this game out aren't very good."

Flaw – Ask how hard something is

"What I would prefer to do is just run the ball the last couple of plays, let the clock run out, and go home. It should be an easy eight to

ten yards a play, which, as you know, is well above the league average per rush and will help with the stats."

Quarterback: "But that will guarantee that we lose the game," the quarterback pleads. "We can't just give them the win without a fight!"

Head Coach: "Settle down. You need to think about the rest of the team. The receivers are already feeling bad about all of the passes that they've dropped, and I'm afraid one more would really damage their self-image. And if you haven't noticed, our pass protection exposes some weaknesses along the offensive line. Not only that, but our running back needs only three more yards to reach a hundred for the first time in his career. I think we all can agree that's a milestone that would really make him feel good about the game. It's a success that we could all enjoy as a team. Besides, have you seen our defense? They are really, really tired, and if you score, they would be forced to go back out and try to stop their offense again. Not only that, but they are planning on having dinner as a group tonight as part of an off-site team-building initiative, and if the game goes into overtime, they might lose their reservation."

KEY – Does this make sense?

- *It isn't about the feelings of the players; it's about winning the game.*

➢ Consider this business basic from a purely selfish perspective. Without profit, there are no jobs, health benefits, paid vacations, bonuses, retirement plans, or promotions. In short, no paychecks, no careers.

    o   Whether you choose to acknowledge or ignore it, the investors in your company, be it a publicly traded or private firm, do not have as their primary objective to ensure that you receive a paycheck regardless of the financial viability of the organization.
- They invested because they expect a return.

    o   They are ***paying you*** because they expect a return from your efforts.
- If you own the business, this isn't merely a concept; it is a crystal clear fact of life.

KEY - Business 101

The coach goes into the General Manager's office for a brief discussion after the first day of training camp and goes straight to the subject that they were both hoping to avoid.

Head Coach: *"I know that we drafted him in the first round, and he's a great young man, but he's due a five million dollar roster bonus in two weeks, and I can't see how we can make that kind of financial commitment to a running back that is going to be third string at best. I'm planning on calling him into my office this evening to release him."*

G.M.: *"I'll get on the phones tonight and contact every team outside of our division. They're only going to pay him what he's worth, but I know several teams that aren't as deep at running back as we are, and might be interested in him as an experienced backup."*

KEY – Be a professional

Head Coach: *"You realize that the press is going to give us some grief for wasting a first-round pick once the news is out."*

G.M.: *"Let's be honest. As it turns out, it was a wasted pick. Regardless of what the press thinks, the objective is to win games, and he isn't helping us achieve that. We need to invest that money in a player who can help us win games."*

KEY – Facts are stubborn things

➢ If your organization fails to deliver quality results, eventually, the investors will pull their money out and find a business that can deliver better numbers. In our impatient world where investors are seeking fast returns, the rapidly expanding number of opportunities means that the time horizon for producing solid profits is steadily shrinking, and as a manager, you are paid to adjust.

KEY – Never get too comfortable

I once heard a coach sum this up by informing the players on his team that they weren't only competing with each other for playing time and roster positions, they were competing against anyone else he could find that would improve the team.

o In the global economy, you are competing for those investment dollars not only within your own industry and country, but against any other company who can provide a better return, anywhere in the world.

- This is also true within an organization, where departments compete over increasingly scarce resources.
  o It may sound cold, but the only reason that they have employed you is because they believe that they can make more money with you there, than without you there.

KEY – Facts are stubborn things

- Are you worth your compensation?
- Do you even know if you are worth your compensation?
➤ Many professionals in business are quick to reply that profit is absolutely essential; however, they can't help but follow up with "But…"
  o There are no buts.
  o Profit is *the* objective.
    - Do it honestly.
    - Be a good member of the community.
    - Be fair to your employees.
    - Be fair to your customers.
  o Never forget the first rule; you must make money, period.

KEY - Business 101

- *Your team must win.*

  o Do the right things.
  o Make the hard decisions.
  o Your objective must be to run a first-class company that delivers bottom line results at the same time.

It makes no sense for a team to run a first-class organization and lose year after year. They must run a class team and consistently win. These are not mutually exclusive objectives. Succeeding in one area is not an excuse for failing at the other. If the team fails at either aspect:

- *The fans will rebel and stop buying tickets.*
- *The best free agents will sign with the competition.*
- *Personnel changes will be demanded.*
- *The team will never become a serious competitor until it starts winning.*

After the last practice of training camp, the newly hired Head Coach called everyone around him at the center of the field.

Head Coach: Pointing to a rookie safety fighting for one of the last roster spots on the team, "In one sentence, what is the most important aspect of your job?"

Safety: Nervously, he steps to the center of the circle. "On pass plays I have deep responsibility if we are in a zone, the tight end if we are in man to man. If I read run…"

Head Coach: He cuts him off. "That's two sentences."

He then turned to the team and one by one started randomly calling players to the center for their one-sentence job description. Awkwardly, they tried to sum up the specifics of their position, struggling to make sure that they used the right buzz words of their position coaches, fearing that the slightest misstep might land them on the waiver wire the next morning. Finally, after nearly twenty minutes, much to the relief of the rest of the team, the Head Coach stepped back into the center.

Head Coach: "This is a perfect example of why this franchise has had losing seasons for the last five years. From this point forward, everyone in this organization has the exact same job objective, whether you are the quarterback, the kicker, or the person in charge of making sure that my headset is operational during a game. Your job is to help this team win games. You may all have your own particular assignments, but whether you are in the weight room, the film room, or on the practice field running drills, you must never lose focus that your job is to help this team win games."

Chapter **3**

Become a Student of the Game
Know Your Business

Considering the growing complexity of business, it may not be practical to be an expert in all of the disciplines relevant to your organization; however, that cannot be used as an excuse for not continuing to learn all you can about those disciplines. The more knowledge that you have, the better position you will be in to make quality decisions. Unfortunately, your business is not defined by your education or experience. It is a mix of sales, finance, technical, customer service, and logistics, just to name a few. The marketplace is not required to neatly adapt to fit your particular abilities and interests. Your approach will always be influenced by your particular background, but you will become much more effective as you develop knowledge across a variety of disciplines. Only then will you have the capability to truly become an effective manager, not only in your current area of responsibility, but over an entire organization.

> ➢ I find it extremely rare to find someone willing to honestly admit that they don't understand their business.
>> o Generally speaking, most people shy away from self-proclaimed incompetence.

- The problem is, most managers who are incompetent sincerely believe that they understand their business and, as a result, make little or no effort to remedy the situation.

Flaw – Bad management

- In these cases we are dealing with the most destructive kind of bad management: incompetent management.
- These managers can actually turn into company killers if left unchecked.
  - Although there is a tendency to live in denial and believe that these managers are rare, the more companies that I work with, the more prevalent I find them to be.
    - Most companies somehow learn to survive despite these individuals, as opposed to dealing with the problem.
- In many organizations, these bad managers rise to the key positions because the one true talent that they actually possess is the ability to talk a good game, talk about it constantly, and with enthusiasm and conviction.
  - Not only are they capable of convincing themselves of their abilities, they manage to persuade those above them of their talents without the benefit of any tangible evidence to support their confidence.
    - It happens every day in business. People talk themselves into positions even while their obvious lack of any achievement screams the truth about their abilities.
      - You cannot allow words and emotions to replace rationale evaluation.
    - The other half of this flaw is that it cannot be completed unless the person doing the hiring or promoting shares some of the same shortcomings.

- Which also happens more often that most managers would like to admit.

Flaw – Management by fuzzy feeling

The Offensive Coordinator called an emergency meeting shortly after learning from the team doctor that the injury to their starting quarterback, which was thought to be minor, would, in fact, be season ending. Although the normal path to follow would be to promote the number-two quarterback into the starting role, after a lengthy discussion late at night with another player, he is ready to make his creative proposal to the Head Coach.

O.C.:   *"I brought Johnson in with me this morning because I thought that it would help give you some confidence in my recommendation if you heard directly from him."*

Johnson: *"Thanks for including me. I'm really excited about the opportunity to be here." He stands up in his new tailored suit and turns off the lights, revealing a large, colorful image projected on the far wall from his computer. "With our starting quarterback out for the rest of the season, I strongly believe that I should assume the role next Sunday." He pauses for effect. "I think that everyone on the team would acknowledge that week after week I have the most insightful feedback throughout our film sessions, and that a detailed understanding of the game is essential to the success of any quarterback in this league." He flashes up a series of pictures showing himself standing up and pointing during film sessions as music begins to fill the office. "Of my own initiative, last night I took the Wonderlic test, which, as you know, is given to all quarterback prospects coming out of college, and I'm pleased to report that my score was one of the highest in many years."*

O.C.:   *"It's worth noting that his score was much higher than either of the other two quarterbacks on the roster." A chart of Johnson's score compared to the other quarterbacks' flashes up on the wall.*

Johnson: *"I believe that my case for being the starter speaks for itself. Physically, I am the prototypical six foot five inches, and come in at a solid two hundred thirty-seven pounds, which will make me very difficult to bring down in the pocket. Additionally, I run a 4.65-second forty-yard dash, making me one of the fastest quarterbacks in the league." A series of close-up pictures showing him lifting weights in tight clothes begin rapidly flashing across the screen as the music grows louder. "When you combine my physical attributes with my understanding of the offense, and consider my score on the Wonderlic test, I believe that I am the clear choice for the job." The final image shows Johnson superimposed under center with the roar of the crowd filling the Head Coach's office.*

O.C.:   *"Last night, I met with him off-site and was extremely impressed with his grasp of the offense, as well as his thoughts on adjustments we could make before this week's game." The coordinator slides a series of full-color laminated pages across the table with Johnson's changes noted in red. "I realize that this is unprecedented, and we may have to sell it to the rest of the team, but I feel good about it. There aren't many teams in this league with the opportunity to start someone possessing an Ivy League education at quarterback."*

Johnson: *"I've studied defenses my whole life, so I took the liberty of designing a few plays to start the game that I would like to run through with you. I am convinced that I can execute them to perfection." He turns off his computer and flips the lights back on.*

Head coach: "I admit that we certainly aren't getting any useful input from either of the other quarterbacks." He shakes his head as he speaks. "Although, it does concern me to start a linebacker from the practice squad. Particularly considering that he has never actually played the position at any level."

KEY – Does this make sense?

Where is the evidence that he can lead the offense? Does anyone even know if he can throw the ball? Your next opponent will not be impressed with his ability to put on a convincing presentation.

- *Examine his history for evidence that would point to his probable success.*

➤ In exactly the same manner, where is the evidence that a prospective manager can perform the job?
   o Examine their history for evidence that would point to probable success.
      ▪ Never rely on the emotion of the moment — think.
   o If a company allows itself to be talked into an individual for a key position, they are deservingly left with a manager that:
      ▪ Has convinced themselves of their own greatness.
      ▪ Has the ability to convince others of their greatness.
      ▪ Has risen to a level in the company where they can inflict significant damage.
         • Not just the ability to, given time, they will inflict damage.
➤ The best way to identify these "company killers" is to create a brief test similar to the one below:

MANAGEMENT TEST 101

a. Finance:
  i. Your most profitable product line is?
  ii. Your least profitable product line is?
  iii. What is your current profit trend?
  iv. What is your cash projection for the current year?

b. Sales:
  i. Who is your largest customer?
  ii. Who are your key competitors?
  iii. What are your strengths and weakness relative to these competitors?
  iv. What product lines offer the greatest opportunity for growth?
  v. What product lines face the greatest threats?

c. Technical:
  i. Describe or demonstrate your three best-selling products or services.
  ii. Describe the most important product/service currently in development.

d. Personnel:
  i. How many employees does the company have?
  ii. Which areas will need more or less employees based on future projections?

> ➤ To the manager that actually is competent, these questions will seem woefully inadequate, which, of course, they are.
> o However, this is all the detail that you need to make your potential bad managers frighteningly obvious.
>   ▪ If you're brave, give the test to your current managers, but be aware that if you don't like what you see, you will need to deal with it.

- *How about if the Head Coach hired his staff by emotions rather than evidence?*

Head Coach: *"Our new offensive coordinator may have a basketball background, and I'll admit really doesn't know much about football right now, but he's a good guy, has a great education, and I'm sure that he will be able to figure it out. I realize that a lot of fans are going to question his decision to keep seven quarterbacks and no running backs on the roster, but hey, he's a smart guy. Besides, I feel good about him, and now that I've made my decision, I'm standing by him."*

KEY – Does this make sense?

- ➤ In most cases, the answers incompetent managers give to your basic test will not simply be wrong, they won't even make sense.
  - o This will rarely stop them from explaining their answers at length, making their incompetence even more apparent for anyone paying attention.
    - ▪ Yes, these people are frequently promoted regardless of their incompetence. As noted earlier, those doing the promoting frequently fail to make the decisions based on relevant criteria.
- ➤ These managers may be key members of your company.
  - o They probably are key members of your company.
- ➤ These managers may be long-term employees.
  - o They probably are long-term employees.
- ➤ These managers may be in charge of key initiatives.
  - o They probably are in charge of key initiatives.
- ➤ If they can't answer the simple test questions, they aren't leaders, and they aren't up to the task, regardless of what the task might be.
  - o Your business cannot afford to promote these individuals.
    - ▪ Furthermore, your business cannot afford to employ these individuals.
  - o It might be time for you to make some difficult decisions.
    - ▪ That is precisely what you are paid to do.

➤ If you truly want to be a leader in your organization, it's not enough to know the:
  o Financials
  o Products/Service
  o Markets, etc.
    ▪ You need to have an understanding of all areas.
    ▪ By understanding your business, and I mean thoroughly understanding your business.
  o If it sounds like a lot, it is. There is a reason why very few people actually are good business leaders — it's hard work, and it never stops.

KEY – Never get too comfortable

  ▪ This includes knowing your employees, customers, markets, competitors, and suppliers.
    • There aren't any substitutions, excuses, or short cuts.

The wide receiver fighting for a spot on the team knows that he needs to cut two-tenths of a second off his forty-yard dash time before the start of training camp. If he wants to succeed, he can't put forth a partial effort. He must:

- *Maximize his effort in the weight room.*
  o *Learn the proper weight training routine to maximize speed.*
- *Maximize his efforts on the track.*
  o *Work with an expert on speed to ensure that his workout and techniques are optimal.*
- *Adopt a strict diet to reach his ideal weight for speed.*

If he wants to be successful, he cannot afford to become an expert in only one area; he needs to learn everything he can about improving his speed.

➢ You cannot sell your company, or yourself, short, and only understand part of your business if you are going to be a leader in your organization.

    o If you are in finance, it's natural that would be the area of your expertise, and that's fine. However, that is not an excuse for not having a working knowledge of sales, engineering, materials, markets, or whatever the key aspects of your organization might be.

        ▪ If you choose not to move beyond your comfort zone, you simply become a highly replaceable employee, and in today's competitive environment, that is precisely what you will likely become — replaced.

We have the same expectations from the Head Coach. He needs to know which offensive plays and formations work, and don't work, against each opponent. He needs to know what defensive calls give them the best opportunity for success. To do this, he must understand the strengths and weaknesses of the other team, as well as the game situation. The better he understands all aspects of the game, the better chance he has to put his players in a position to make plays and win the game.

➢ These same expectations are essential from any manager. Furthermore, how can you run your company without a detailed, thorough understanding of your business?

    o You can't.

➢ Know your game.

    o Understand all aspects.

    o Be in a position to intelligently provide input.

        ▪ In the real world, simply being smart is worthless; you must be smart as it relates to your business.

Within each of these areas, we expect that coaches will understand the intricacies of the game, how they will affect the future of the team, and after a game, why they did or didn't work. The individual coordinators may be making the calls from play to play; however, it would be irresponsible for the Head Coach not to be integral to the formation of the overall game plan, and step in if their strategy isn't working and changes need to be made. Although the coach may have come up through the offensive ranks, he must know when a defensive change is needed or a new kicker needs to be brought in. He must have the knowledge to help the entire team develop and maintain a competitive level of play if he is going to be successful.

Chapter 4

The Team Philosophy
Arrive at Your Destination on Purpose

M any managers fall into the shortsighted trap of allowing the urgency of the daily circumstances swirling around them to unintentionally determine the future of their business. Every organization is constantly evolving; it's just a matter of whether they are changing based on analysis and planning, or unconsciously stumbling toward some unknown destination, blindly hoping that when they arrive, they are still solvent. If you don't know your destination, it is impossible to create a road map for your organization, or even determine if you should be traveling by roller skate or jet plane. Once you step back from the chaos and develop a clear vision for the direction of your company, you can then begin the process of creating a road map detailing the specifics of the journey ahead. With the road map established, it then becomes essential to ensure that everyone has a copy of the map, and understands the importance of the destination and the path that will be followed. Then, as new roads are built, or unexpected construction creates delays, you can make adjustments to take advantage of opportunities, or avoid the inevitable traffic jams. Without a clear destination, it is impossible to know which direction to turn as the organization navigates through the stresses and surprises of the working day. Every organization is on a journey, including yours. Know where you are going, why you are going there, and the path that will lead you there.

- ➤ In our rapidly evolving business world, it's impossible to help any organization reach its potential without a detailed, well thought out, long-term plan.
  - o With the speed of change facing managers today, failing to develop a clear direction for your organization is no longer just a matter of limiting your potential; it's a matter of survival.
    - ▪ The all too common practice of depending on luck to move your organization forward is not only increasingly ineffective, it's irresponsible.

Flaw – Bad management

- ➤ In the past, bad management was frequently able to muddle along, and even if the company consistently underachieved, at least they usually survived.
  - o Going forward, that will not be an alternative as competition intensifies.
    - ▪ The new world is going to demand that you professionally manage your business, and the punishment for not stepping up will be an inability to compete.

KEY – Never get too comfortable

- o The opening of the global marketplace has meant that the windows of opportunity are more numerous than at any time in history.
  - ▪ Simultaneously, because of the corresponding

increase in competition, these same windows of opportunity will open and close more rapidly than most managers are accustomed to.

➢ The days of sitting back to see what markets materialize are over.

    o When an opportunity presents itself, you must already be in position to take advantage of it, or a competitor will step in, and the window will rapidly be slammed shut in your face.

    o In the same manner, when threats present themselves, you must be able to immediately make the necessary adjustments to avoid irreparable damage to your organization.

Flaw – Debating if change is good or bad

Head Coach: *"Smith's agent just called, and although he's had larger offers, he likes our offensive approach and coaching staff, and will concede one less year on the contract if we match the twelve-million-dollar signing bonus."*

G.M.: *"That's great news! I never considered that he might give up that fifth year to come here." The excitement is obvious in his voice. "It has been a long time since we were able to land a major free agent. Once news is out that he's signed, we're going to get consideration from several other players still on the market that would significantly upgrade the team. This could turn us into a serious contender next season. We need to get everyone together and see what we can do to clear enough cap room to sign him. I'll get on it first thing in the morning. It's going to take some difficult decisions, but in his case, we need to find a way to work through it."*

Head Coach: *"That's no good; his agent is holding on the line to talk through the details with you right now. If we can't* *commit to freeing the space immediately, his next call will be to Chicago accepting their offer, and instead of having him on our roster, he will be lining up against us twice a year."*

➤ Reemphasizing how I started this chapter, there is no way a manager in the current business environment can establish priorities without having a plan with clear objectives established for the future.

    o Many managers continue to live in the past and look no further than the end of the day, living in denial that they are putting both themselves, and their business, in jeopardy.

The offensive coordinator examines the defensive set and quickly signals out a late play change. Noting that their alignment doesn't have anyone over the center, and that the middle linebacker is seven yards off the line of scrimmage, he decides to take advantage of the situation and run a quarterback sneak. The quarterback pauses briefly as he glances at the defense, which is indeed conceding three or four yards up the middle, considers that it's third and fourteen, shrugs his shoulders, and runs the play signaled in to avoid a confrontation with their hot-headed offensive coordinator.

Flaw – Bad management

➤ It's arrogant to assume that you can make intelligent short-term decisions without knowing the long-term goals.

After the game, the quarterback meets with his supervisor, the Offensive Coordinator, for a performance review:

O.C.:   *"I like the way that you execute the quarterback sneak; however, looking down at the objectives that we both agreed on at the beginning of the season, it's becoming apparent that you are going to fall well short of your first down target for the season.* "

Quarterback: *"You can't expect me to pick up first downs when you call plays that aren't capable of gaining the necessary yardage."*

O.C.: *Visibly upset. "Look, I'll worry about the play calling, you worry about picking up first downs." He makes a note to pass along to the Head Coach concerning the quarterback's reluctance to accept responsibility.*

➤ Unfortunately, many companies allow planning for the future to become overrun with critical demands that need to be dealt with in the next minute, hour, or day.
  o You cannot allow the crisis of the moment to become an excuse for neglecting long-term planning.
    ▪ In the real world, there will always be a crisis of the moment.
    ▪ To be an effective manager, you ___must___ address both.
➤ Every organization has a certain amount of momentum; it's the manager's job, the leader's responsibility, to make sure that:
  o The company is moving in a positive direction.
  o The company is moving fast enough in the right direction.
    ▪ In both cases, direction is the key. Your business is headed somewhere — get there on purpose.

KEY – Be a professional

    ▪ The world is changing much too rapidly to stumble into the future without a plan.
  o You must consistently utilize all of your current resources to ensure the future viability of the organization.
    ▪ Your success today has very little to do with

success in the future.
- o Where are the markets headed for your products and services?
    - Are they expanding?
    - Are they shrinking?
    - Are they disappearing?

Head Coach: *"Based on what we have seen the last couple of plays, there is no way that they can stop us running from this formation," he says to his quarterback as the offense takes the field. "A minimum of five yards a play. We can march straight down the field and punch it into the end zone."*

Quarterback: *"Coach, there's only thirty-seven seconds left in the game."*

KEY – Does this make sense?

- ➤ Specifically, what are your plans to achieve your goals?
    - o Are they realistic?
    - o What resources will be needed?
    - o Is the time frame realistic?
        - What timeline is the market demanding?
    - o Is the plan capital intensive?
        - Is the capital accessible?
    - o Do you have the personnel in place?
    - o Never stop asking questions.

After an exhaustive research project that focused on last year's playoff teams, the coaching staff has committed to running the ball seventy percent of the time next season. Before jumping in and implementing their latest insight, they need to consider if the new direction fits the makeup of the current organization:
- • *Does the team have a quality running back?*

- *Is the offensive line oriented toward the run?*
- *Is there enough depth at key positions in case there is an injury?*
- *Is the Offensive Coordinator an expert at implementing running offenses?*
- *In short, do the abilities of the team meet the demands of the plan?*

➢ If you have determined that your company needs to make a substantive change in strategy, the first priority must be to determine if your staff is capable of implementing the change.
  o Have they been trained?
  o Do they have sufficient experience?
  o Regardless of training and experience, do they have the talent?
    ▪ This isn't a very popular question.
  o Change is never perfect; do you have the kind of personnel who are open to change, and the challenges that invariably accompany it?

Going into the game, the plan was to throw the ball down the field early to back up their linebackers and safeties, who were notorious for creeping up toward the line of scrimmage. By moving their defense deeper, it would open up the running game, where the real strength of the offense was. However, during the first quarter, the quarterback was sacked four times, their defense was blitzing on nearly every play, and it was obvious that they had no respect for the passing game.

They could remain committed to establishing the running game, but with eight defensive players in the box on every play, some changes had to be made in the play selection. Coming out in the second quarter, they adjusted by mixing in some draw and screen plays to slow down some of the pressure. The overall game plan remained the same, but the play calling needed to reflect what was taking place on the field. The players needed to keep focused on the game plan, but also had to be aware that the path to get there had changed, their assignments had been revised, and everyone needed to make the adjustments together if they were going to be successful.

Chapter 5

Play with a Purpose
Hoping for the Best Isn't a Plan

Always have hope. It is exactly the kind of attitude that you need permeating every facet of your organization. In the same measure, I firmly believe that optimism is essential for any leader to be successful. However, despite all of this positive thinking, it is equally imperative that your optimism be constantly reexamined to ensure that it has a rational basis. You must plan, execute, follow up, and adapt your business strategy in a manner that results in creating a foundation for optimism. Feeling positive about the future of your business without good reason isn't optimism, it's the naiveté found in businesses being managed by hope.

➢ Can you think of anything that makes less sense than hoping that things work out without having a clear plan in place to make it happen?
  o That represents a plan that is nothing short of irrational management.

Flaw – Management by fuzzy feeling

- ▪ Replacing a business plan with hoping for the best is about as fuzzy as it gets.
  - ○ You are participating in a highly competitive world where your adversaries begin every day actively intent on working against your best interests.
    - ▪ Sorry, no nice fuzzy way to say it. Your competitors are constantly developing plans where they succeed, and you fail.

KEY – Never get too comfortable

Not-so-great coaching quotes:

- *"I hope that they didn't watch any of last week's game films and realize that we can't run the ball."*
- *"I hope that our quarterback is out of the hospital in time for the game."*
- *"I hope that the team read the new playbook that we emailed out to everyone after practice last night."*
- *"I hope that our corners realize that we are going to blitz the safeties on every third down. I just know that it won't be my fault because I text messaged everyone twice last week."*
- *"Every time we blitzed, they scored. I hope it works better in the second half."*

KEY – Does this make sense?

Actions that are routinely carried out every day in business reveal themselves as absurd under game situations. Professional coaches are constantly searching for weaknesses, strengths, and tendencies that can be exploited throughout the game to create an advantage for their team. They would never consider sending their team out on the field without every player having identical, current game plans, or directing them to report back after the game regarding how everything went. They remain fully engaged with their team throughout the game.

➤ Despite this, hope as the centerpiece of a company's strategic plan is extraordinarily common. Going further, regardless of the complete lack of logic of this approach, it is the most common plan that I encounter.
  o Even many of the formal plans that companies are proud to put forth are based more on hope than substance if you take the time to look below the cleverly constructed words and colorful charts so eloquently presented.
    ▪ In many companies, the effective use of PowerPoint has replaced analysis and cognitive thought.
      • It's easier.

Flaw – Ask how hard something is

➤ Hope, as a plan, is the very definition of bad management; or to be more precise, no management.
  o If you are still confused, refer to the prior point.
➤ The convenient outcome of this strategy is that you don't have to worry about reality, at least for a while.
  o Because you have chosen to ignore reality.
➤ My experience has been that prototypical managers committed to pursuing the hope philosophy have frighteningly similar habits:
  o When things aren't going well, nothing changes, virtually guaranteeing that the situation will worsen.
  o When things are going well, nothing changes, virtually guaranteeing that the organization will find itself struggling in the future.

- Note that the hope strategy involves:
  - Never taking substantive action.
  - The organization consistently deteriorates.
➤ If you want good things to happen, you must stop hoping and start to plan, execute, follow up, and adjust.

KEY – Be a professional

o If your plan is to get lucky, put yourself in the best possible position to get lucky.
  - Note how often good luck, and bad luck, follows the same people throughout life.
➤ Once you have established a plan, that represents only the start of the commitment.
  o Actions need to be specific and coordinated with the overall business plan.
  o Employees need to clearly demonstrate the rationale that their plans will achieve the stated objectives.
    - Why will they work?
    - When will they be completed?
    - How will they be accomplished?
      - Only then will you be in a position to support them in reaching their objectives, or make changes as new opportunities and threats surface.
  o Finally, never make the mistake of assuming that actions will be accomplished just because you were told so.
    - You are responsible for following up.
  o Do not back a plan that isn't actually a plan. Insist on your employees developing and maintaining real plans.
    - You are responsible for continually replacing hope with substance.

The team cannot have a play that merely calls for gaining five yards on third down. It isn't even enough to say that they have a running play with the objective of gaining five yards. If that's the play, the team will fail. The players need specific direction regarding the details of the play, and what their responsibilities are, if they want a realistic chance of gaining the necessary yardage. With every play, the responsibility of the coaching staff is to make sure that the team is fully prepared to be successful.

- *How will the play be executed, and precisely what is expected from each player?*
- *Do the players understand their assignments?*
- *Do the players' objectives match the objectives of the play?*
- *Are the players properly prepared for their respective assignments?*
  - o *Even if properly trained, do they have the ability to fulfill their requirements?*
- *Does the play match up with the circumstances on the field?*
- *What happened the last time that they ran the play?*
  - o *Did they learn anything?*
  - o *Do they need to make any adjustments?*
  - o *Has the defense made any adjustments?*

➢ Take time to think. In many cases, thinking will prove to be your most significant competitive advantage.

KEY – Be a professional

- o Then, take action based on what you have learned.
  - ▪ Know your market.
  - ▪ Know your customers.
  - ▪ Know your competitors.
  - ▪ Know your strengths.
  - ▪ Know your weaknesses.
- o Implement a plan that is detailed, defendable, and flexible.

49

- Follow up and adapt to changes as they develop.
➤ Hope is a terrible plan. A wonderful sounding ideal, but a terrible plan exercised by only the weakest of leaders.
  o When management doesn't know what to do.
  o When management has no real plan.
  o When management neglects their responsibility.

Flaw – Bad management

- For everyone's sake, don't just hope — take action.

The General Manager and the Head Coach sat alone in the film room at the close of the season. They both realized that retirements and injures were going to significantly alter the makeup of their team going into the next season.

Head Coach: "We have a good group of veterans remaining on the roster, but not enough depth to be competitive, and several of those players will be retiring over the next couple of seasons. If we play to the maximum of our potential and pick up a couple of free agents, we might get lucky and go eight-eight the next couple of years."

G.M.: "We both know that's not acceptable for this franchise. The expectations are just too high."

Head Coach: "Our personal expectations are even higher, but that doesn't change where we are at this moment."

G.M.: "The objective of this franchise is to win championships. If the current roster isn't capable of meeting that standard, then we need to make changes and start building toward that goal."

Head Coach: "*I think that it's time to make a few trades to move toward a younger roster, load up on draft picks, and clear some room under the salary cap so that we can aggressively target a couple of key free agents. If we clearly detail our needs, avoid getting caught up in the emotions of chasing high-profile players we don't need, and stick to our plan, we can be back in the hunt within a couple of seasons.*"

G.M.: "*I agree, but rebuilding won't be an excuse for not being competitive next season. We can't lose sight during the off-season that we must put a quality team on the field even while we are retooling the roster.*"

Chapter **6**

Playing to Your Strengths
Constantly Reevaluate and Adapt

Y ou now have a quality plan, hope has been replaced with substance, and your company is ready to confidently move forward. What you must now be constantly aware of is that business in the modern world shifts without warning or mercy, and if you are not in a position to rapidly adapt, you are likely to be punished. The adjustments made to win a game in an unexpected snowstorm are critical to the team's success, but the ultimate goal remains winning championships. As a leader, you must keep your vision focused on the long-term goals of the organization, while remaining keenly aware of any fundamental market developments that may render your plans obsolete. Creating a high-quality, realistic plan is essential to the long-term success of any organization. At the same time, it is becoming increasingly imperative that your plan represents a living document that has the flexibility to adapt to any new realities that suddenly appear on the horizon.

➢ Things change.
   o You must be aware that ignoring change **_will_** result in your demise.
➢ The purpose of this brief chapter is to emphasize that once you

have faced reality, the changes you make must continually be incorporated into your business plan.

- o Your plan must be represented in a document that is constantly being adjusted to reflect the ever-changing realities of the marketplace.
  - ▪ It should be full of worn pages, revisions, sticky notes, and red lines by the time the next formal planning cycle comes around.

KEY – Be a professional

- ➤ Far too often, I see companies following the identical nonsensical planning cycle:
  - o The financial department emails the forms out to the management staff with final submission and presentation dates.
  - o Sales scrambles to assemble projections targeting the lowest numbers that they think they can get away with, knowing that ultimately they will be raised to an already predetermined level without their input.
  - o Engineering and product development will request as much investment as possible without completely embarrassing themselves, knowing that it will be slashed without their input.
    - ▪ And so goes the process from department to department.
  - o What does the company get? Exactly what they deserve.
    - ▪ A plan that top management proudly showcases as the future of the business.
    - ▪ A plan where the employees will be held accountable for the results, even though they know it's doomed even before the ink dries.
      - • Many managers won't even bother to show their subordinates the final copy because

they realize that it would prove demotivating.

- A plan that is more likely to be used as a disciplinary stick, rather than as a management tool and means of incentive.
- A plan that is put on the shelf to gather dust until the next cycle.
  - A few brief paragraphs will be dedicated to describing why the last plan failed to develop as promised.
- A plan that has nothing to do with the decisions made on a day-to-day basis within the business.
- A plan that is a waste of time and source of frustration to the employees.

The key members of the management and coaching staff gathered together for their annual off-site planning meeting the week before the commencement of training camp:

G.M.:　　　*"I don't think that any of us are satisfied with consecutive seven win seasons, and justifiably, ownership is demanding significant improvements. As a result, I have taken the initiative to establish a set of objectives for the upcoming season. Offensively, we need to commit to a minimum of twenty-four points a game, with at least two touchdowns coming through the air. Defensively, we are targeting to keep opponents below twenty points a game by focusing on holding them under one hundred yards rushing each week. As you can all see, this kind of performance will result in an undefeated season." He is obviously proud of his proposal.*

Head Coach: "Those are admirable goals…" He is trying to pick his words carefully. "But you lost our entire starting backfield to free agency, two of our key offensive linemen retired, and as we discussed at the close of last season, we needed to fill some big holes defensively, yet failed to sign anyone. I really think that we need to take this season one game at a time and focus on developing some of our young players."

G.M.:   *"That's simply not good enough, and frankly, I'm disappointed in your reluctance to come on board."*

O.C.:   *"The players will know that those are unrealistic objectives with our current roster. The goals, and the coaching staff, won't be taken seriously."*

G.M.:   *"I can promise each one of you that if this coaching staff is not prepared to enthusiastically sign up to this plan right now, not all of us will be in this room a year from now." He pounds the table. "Now, who's with me?"*

It doesn't matter which coaches sign up, or what their level of enthusiasm is. The one certainty the General Manager has created is that the coaching staff will immediately begin reestablishing contacts within their coaching network. The General Manager is out of touch, the team will fail to meet the unrealistic objectives, and there will be changes as key members of the staff find new positions with more stable management.

> ➢ Utilizing your resources to develop a plan that isn't a realistic, integral part of your business can only be described as poor management.

Flaw – Bad management

- o Actually, my favorite category, mindless management.
  - ▪ You wasted time.
  - ▪ Created frustrated employees.

- Produced numbers and plans that are disingenuous at best, realistically, dishonest.

Flaw – Lack of integrity

➢ The global markets have resulted in the creation of more opportunities than at any time in history, but you must put yourself in a position to react quickly to take advantage of them.
  o You must be prepared to make the necessary adjustments.
➢ The opposite is also true; there are more threats than at any time in history, and trouble comes fast and with little compassion for the problems it creates.
  o Products that once had a ten-year life span now have a one-year life span, and may disappear tomorrow without any warning. There is no point in hoping that it doesn't happen to your company.

KEY – Never get too comfortable

➢ Make your plans, then have the courage to say that something is wrong, or that the basis has changed.
  o Markets change.
  o New competitors enter or leave the market.
  o The economy changes.
  o Cost structures change.
  o Oil goes to seventy dollars a barrel.
    - For some companies, this may have an immediate impact that could result in significant profit upside, or conversely, represent a threat that could destroy the business.

KEY – Facts are stubborn things

- o Hurricanes devastate a region.
    - ▪ Consider the company that fails to adjust to the reality of a hurricane while their operations are under three feet of water.

The starting quarterback went down for the season on the final play of the game, and his backup is a rookie with no game experience. Is the rookie ready, or do they need to bring in a veteran for a year while he continues to mature? Does he even have the potential to be a starter in the league? The team's league-leading passing attack just lost their five-time pro bowl leader on a single play, and as a result, everything has changed. The Head Coach has suddenly been put into the position of needing to reconsider their entire offensive philosophy.

- ➢ Your sales manager of twenty years just took an unexpected early retirement.
    - o Is there someone on the staff that is honestly up to task? (If not, your planning wasn't very good.)
        - ▪ Things just changed. Going about business as if nothing has changed is irresponsible.

Flaw – Debating if change is good or bad

- o If something significant has changed, ***management is responsible*** to adapt.
    - ▪ And, everything is changing.
- ➢ Developing a plan is an essential starting point, but you must take the next step and take responsibility for committing to a plan that can be used as the centerpiece of driving your company forward. This requires that it not only be adaptable to meet changes, but even more critically, that you are personally adaptable.

With some quick thinking and hard work, the Head Coach was able to make changes to the game plan and escape with victory despite the weather conditions. The newspapers are proclaiming his genius for turning what was expected to be a high-scoring game into a battle for field position. The accolades of the day make for good reading, but the expectations will quickly turn toward winning the game next Sunday.

It's not the good Head Coach that remains locked into a game plan regardless of the circumstances. The coach must be aware of potential opportunities and obstacles, and then make the proper adjustments as the game unfolds. The keys are preparation, knowledge, and the willingness to make the necessary changes. It requires constantly being aware that plans will always need to change once they crash into reality.

Chapter 7

<u>A Quality Roster</u>
Hire and Keep the Best Employees

I consistently find the largest disparities between what management claims and what they actually do, as it relates to personnel issues. Companies are filled with thoughtful philosophies that are propped up by carefully constructed mission statements and meticulously crafted values proclamations. The conflict arises when they are ultimately revealed as shallow commitments that represent little more than a fresh coat of paint on a rusted-out car that hasn't run in years. Managers persist in believing that if they can just develop the right words, they can avoid committing to the constant reinforcement of their stated positions with actions. It doesn't take many probing questions for those self-righteous claims of "employee first" to become buried in hypocrisy. Job descriptions are developed to fulfill ISO, or some other system requirements, but typically have little to do with what the individual is actually doing. One-sided objectives, performance bars set unrealistically high, or, conversely, set low enough to accommodate anyone that might be thrown into the cubicle. Do a great job, get a four-percent raise. Go through the motions, a three-percent raise.

Burdensome as it may seem, saying that you care requires that you actually care. You must care about the company. You must care about the individual. You must care enough to insist that both the company and the person strive to realize certain levels of performance. You must put both the company and the employee in the best possible position to succeed. Place the bar where it actually belongs, not where it creates the least amount of work or conflict.

➢ Every organization that I have ever worked with claims that hiring and keeping the best employees is an essential ingredient of their corporate philosophy. It's the standard boilerplate personnel philosophy that is regurgitated by smiling executives everywhere.
   o The reality in the normal course of business is that they settle for adequate employees, and do little more than hope that their good employees remain with the organization.
      ▪ It's a much easier path to follow in the short term.

Flaw – Ask how hard something is

➢ Success is a direct result of your people. It's imperative that management commits not only to good employees, but also equally as important, good people.
   o A company and its systems are not capable of accomplishing anything on their own. They require people, good people, and that doesn't happen by accident.
➢ More than just a philosophy, managers at all levels that I have worked with agree that good employees are ***at least*** twice as productive as so-called adequate employees.
   o My personal experience has been that this is a very conservative estimate, and it's not just a matter of output, it's the quality of the output, and the manner in which they go about producing it.
      ▪ On the flip side, the same small group of employees will repeatedly create the vast majority of your personnel headaches.

There is a reason why an all-pro player can demand a salary several multiples of the average player who is lining up next to them. Supply and demand has established that the players who can produce consistently superior results are worth the money because they are difficult to find and, even more importantly, have the ability to deliver wins. Conversely, in the world of salary caps, the same player clearly understands that if his results don't live up to expectations, it's likely that the team will not only question his compensation, but may even choose to end the relationship.

- o Despite this knowledge, when the need arises, too many businesses fall into the "filling the hole" syndrome.
  - ▪ This is the natural outcome when the person responsible for the hiring is too lazy to invest the effort into doing a quality job.

KEY – Never get too comfortable

During a disastrous practice, the team lost both starting safeties to injury for the remainder of the season. Even before the practice was over, the Head Coach was on his cell phone to the General Manager.

Head Coach: *"I need a couple of safeties, and I need them fast."*

G.M.: *"I've been watching player movements over the past couple of weeks, and quite frankly, there aren't many quality safeties with game experience available right now. I'll work to get several here by the end of the week for a workout, but short-term you may want to consider moving a couple of your corners to safety. While you're doing that, I'll start exploring trade options."*

Head Coach: *"I really need someone here for tomorrow's practice. Just get me a couple of players with some experience anywhere in the secondary, even if it's just at the college level. I would prefer to plug in a new player rather than* *disrupt practice and try moving the entire defensive backfield around.*"

KEY – Does this make sense?

- o Management isn't honestly committed to hiring the best employees.
    - ▪ What they truly believe, but won't say, is that anyone can do the job.
- ➢ Another concern in the world of streamlining and cutbacks is that managers fear that if they don't move quickly, someone from "above" will decide that the position isn't necessary.
    - o The person doing the hiring should be the one actually considering the relevancy of replacement every time that there is a vacancy.
        - ▪ Does the position increase the profitability of the organization?
            - • You should never fill any position without asking this question.

KEY - Business 101

- ▪ Take the time, and the pain, to find people that you believe in.
- o To avoid the habit of filling the hole, ask these two questions:
    - ▪ Is this individual a good fit for the next five years?
    - ▪ Would I trust my career to this person?
        - • If you are comfortable with these two questions, you can then start the process of evaluating their credentials.
- ➢ In the new global economy, managing personnel is a discipline

where you have an opportunity to establish, and maintain, a significant competitive advantage.

- o Hire people you believe not only can perform the job but, additionally, employees who will have a positive influence on those around them.
    - Establish the standard with your employees that you expect them to follow when they are hiring.
- o This demands that you draw on the largest pool of potential talent every time that you fill a position.
    - Sexism and racism are only capable of limiting your organization. By default, you are eliminating individuals who could improve your company.

Flaw – Lack of integrity

- • You cannot afford to draw from a limited pool of talent.
- • You cannot afford to employ anyone who routinely utilizes only a limited pool of talent.
- o This means that we must be committed to creating a talent pool as large as possible if we are going to compete, and this starts with refusing to allow circumstances to block anyone from getting a quality education who is willing to work for one.
    - This isn't a social position; it's an unavoidable economic reality.

KEY – Facts are stubborn things

It would be impossible for our football team to remain competitive if they only drafted players from the Big Ten, Big East, or Southwest

Conference. They would be excluding too many quality players who could make the team better. By limiting the talent pool, they would put their team at a competitive disadvantage against every team that evaluates all available players. Professional football teams are involved in a constant search to find the next potential source of prospects, not limit them. They must have the best eleven players on the field at any given time. The only time that the coach's brother-in-law would be added to the roster would be if he honestly earned his place on the team. In a competitive situation, there is no room for any other philosophy. The quarterback doesn't care if the left tackle is African-American, white, Asian, or some mix of races. Although we are dealing with the ultimate male-dominated world of professional football, he doesn't care if it's a man or woman. He doesn't care if they are attractive or not, tall or short, young or old, bald or have a ponytail hanging out the back of their helmet. In the heat of the game, the only thing that the quarterback cares about is that the best possible person is protecting his blind side, and that requires considering the largest possible talent pool that the scouts can identify.

- o When you see a competitor that utilizes only part of the potential workforce, you should be considering that a competitive advantage. Even if at times it may be cultural, as markets expand around the world — i.e., it's traditional to only hire men — they are providing you with an advantage and you must take advantage of it.
  - ▪ Identifying good employees requires that you don't make compromises.

KEY – Be a professional

- ➢ Hire positive people.
  - o Good employees and negative attitudes are diametrically opposed.
    - ▪ People are either negative or positive.

- Warning — negative people will always refer to themselves as realists.
- Hire people who want to be challenged, and have the capability to grow and adapt.
  - In the new world, management must keep expectations high for everyone in the organization.
  - You cannot afford to lower the essential standards of the organization so that anyone can reach them.

It's the ultimate red flag when evaluating players for draft day — the player who never quite lived up to expectations in college. A few pounds overweight, too many off-field distractions, or a questionable work ethic. All of the physical gifts God can bestow, but lacking a consistent commitment to excellence. Most teams have learned the hard way that players either have good character, or poor character, and in most cases it's impossible to salvage a player lacking character.

At the combine, the General Manager and the Head Coach stood taking notes on all of the prospects, but their attention kept returning to the raw but supremely talented quarterback, who had probably come out a year too early considering his off-field issues. Generally considered a second-round pick due to his well-publicized baggage, they held the fifteenth pick in the first round, and didn't have another selection until the third round.

Head Coach: "He clearly has the most upside of anyone on the field."

G.M. "At the same time, his reputation carries the most downside. If we pick him in the first round, it would be the highest risk pick that we have ever made."

Head Coach: "Can we move down and take him a little later to minimize our exposure?"

G.M. "Normally, I would say yes, but you and I both know that he's a Chicago native, and they are going to take him at twenty-seven, regardless of where the experts say he should go. The real issue is, knowing his history, are you prepared to personally invest the required time into the management of his progress?" He turns toward the Head Coach. "Our careers depend on drafting and developing the right players; how many attitudes have either of us been able to change through the years? Can we really afford to take the time away from the other players on the team?"

- o Hire people you believe can not only succeed in an environment with high expectations, but also thrive in it.
- ➤ Once you have managed to hire good people, it's equally essential to keep them.
    - o I firmly believe that keeping good employees starts with *your* character.
        - ▪ Many times, employees don't quit companies, they quit their bosses.
    - o To be an effective leader, you must:
        - ▪ Care about the people that you work with.
        - ▪ Treat the people that you work with fairly.

        - • Don't expect your employees to be content with their compensation being determined by market levels if the executive staff exempts themselves.

Flaw – Lack of integrity

- ▪ It may be impossible to always be in complete agreement; however, the goal has to be to continually align individual and organizational objectives as much as possible.
    - • Openly discuss any areas of potential conflict.
- ▪ Replacing good employees is both time-consuming and painful.

- ➢ The final and most neglected personnel flaw that kills companies is the all too frequent cop-out of not firing "jerks."
  - o I cannot communicate this message any clearer.
  - o Some employees are not just emotional, high maintenance, or even difficult. They are jerks, and they need to be sent on their way.
    - ▪ As nice as it would be to reform everyone, some employees have no interest in changing regardless of what some new philosophy may be proclaiming.

Flaw – Management by fuzzy feeling

- ▪ Fortunately for the managers responsible for these employees, once confronted, jerks are very poor at maintaining their cheerful, cooperative new attitudes, making their insincerity quickly transparent.
  - o If you're not sure who these people are in your organization, either;
    - ▪ You aren't paying attention.
    - ▪ The jerk is you.
  - o Ask around. The same name(s) will just keep surfacing.

This is the receiver who would rather get "his catches," or get into the end zone to perform his latest dance, than win the game. For lack of a better description, let's call him Out of Touch, O.T. This player is so selfish that he has a complete inability to do what's in the best interest of the team. He may produce great individual statistics, but he emotionally exhausts everyone around him and takes the focus off the team's objectives.

- ➢ The most common fear of management in these cases is that "we can't live without them."
  - o Yes, you can.

o Unfortunately, in many companies, these jerks are not only tolerated, but are routinely promoted into powerful positions.

Flaw – Bad management

o Managing their attitude becomes the all-consuming task of everyone sentenced to work with them.
   - These individuals cause others to spend energy trying to avoid confrontations with them, or work around them, rather than focusing their efforts on the needs of the organization.
   - Without exception, these individuals dramatically reduce the efficiency of those forced to interact with them.
o Your responsibility is to influence and inspire those people that you are working with. That starts with credibility, and you **_cannot_** have credibility if you don't deal with the jerks of your organization.
o As noted earlier, my experience has been that I have found only two types of people:
   - Positive
   - Negative
o Jerks are the quintessential negative employees. They are self-centered and always willing to trample on those around them to achieve **_their_** goals.
   - At the core they are supremely selfish — it's all about them.
➢ At one company, I ran across an example of the prototypical jerk and the mandatory management accommodation that kept him propped up, which is worthy of a brief story.

The company had a good employee, whom everyone liked and who was being considered for several promotions that were on the horizon.

During this period, the company moved a new supervisor into the area, and he immediately started creating conflicts with the staff. He was an inflexible prima donna, carrying a constant air of arrogance around the workplace, and always condescending toward those he worked with. His professional habits included unceasing criticism of others, demanding his way in every situation, talking behind the backs of coworkers and subordinates, and the always-professional refusal to acknowledge the person standing next to him if he was unhappy (which was always). All of his bad habits had the recurring theme of an apparent inability to work with women.

When the inevitable complaint came to the area manager, her solution was to allow the employee to directly contact the corporate office to register a formal complaint. By the time the episode was over, everyone had wasted several days, the local office had been in a prolonged, and unnecessary, state of turmoil, the area manager had lost all credibility, multiple corporate staff members had been tied up, and it was resolved in the most predictable manner:

- ➤ The legal department determined that it was unlikely that they were going to be sued.
  - o Job one for any company too weak to deal with their jerks.
- ➤ The employee who was being treated unprofessionally was told that she was just going to have to try harder to get along.
  - o The good employee subsequently left the company.
- ➤ The jerk stayed and received validation of his behavior directly from the corporate office.
  - o The company took a giant step backward.

The irony was that he had been transferred to the new location because of his inability to get along with people at his old location. What a big surprise that he was causing problems; they had already identified him as a jerk, and didn't deal with it. My promise to their management — he will give them another opportunity to deal with his destructive personality in the near future.

KEY – Does this make sense?

G.M.: "We really should cut Smith, but he would blast us in the papers. Do you have any thoughts?"

Head Coach: "I may move him from left to right cornerback to see if he can get along better with the linebacker on that side of the field."

➢ The company that eliminates the jerks who are choking the productivity out of their organization creates a huge competitive advantage.
  o The manager who chooses to accommodate the jerks destroys his or her credibility in dealing with personnel issues professionally, and permanently lowers expectations within the organization.

Professional football represents one of the most uncompromising examples of managing personnel. Everyone's job description is clearly tied to winning games. The requirements for each job aren't determined by what the player can or cannot do, or by what the owner thinks, but rather what is required from the position on the field. Every player understands his role, specifically why his role is critical to the success of the team, and their performance is constantly evaluated against those expectations. If a job description needs to be revised, it's done immediately. While it remains human to like some players better than others, the practice field, the film room, and the results throughout games reveal the best players and push aside personal feelings. The coaching staff invests significant amounts of energy every day into developing potential, but recognize that potential must produce results in a reasonable period of time if the player is going to remain with the team. In franchises that consistently produce winning teams, the jerks, regardless of their raw talent, are shown the door before they can infect the entire team. Although the professional football model of Human Resource Management might prove too inflexible for your business, everyone could learn a lot from their uncompromising approach to assessing the talents and needs of their organization.

- *Be fair.*
- *Be honest.*
- *Have clear job descriptions with reviews based on results.*
- *Have clear organizational goals.*
- *Set the bar high for everyone in the organization.*
  - *Anywhere below winning is unacceptable.*

Chapter **8**

<u>You Can't Win with Penalties</u>
Demand Integrity

There is nothing positive that can come from compromising, or allowing those we work with to compromise, integrity. Rather than it being an assumption that you try to wrap around your business, it must be the core that you build your business around. I find it increasingly concerning how little emphasis values actually receive from company to company, and how most organizations, although they would never verbalize it, appear to be quite comfortable with "most of the time." The inevitable conflict arises from the fact that integrity cannot be compromised on only rare occasions. If an individual or organization isn't fully committed, then they can never be trusted, because it is impossible to determine when the next concession will be made. You must be able to trust those you work with; however, never ignore that trust is a quality that is earned, not randomly bestowed upon someone just because they hold an impressive title.

> ➤ Integrity has evolved into such a taken-for-granted commodity that oftentimes it receives only surface level attention within many organizations.
>> o It seems so obvious that it's rarely discussed, or even acknowledged, within most companies.

- Normal operating procedure is that it is captured within the corporate code of conduct, or even specifically contained in the mission statement. However, words on a piece of paper do not make for a viable company philosophy.
  - Actions, regardless of what is so eloquently printed below your overpriced consultant-designed company logo, make for the real company philosophy.
- ➢ Integrity starts with dealing honestly with your suppliers, customers, and employees. You must be able to trust the people you are working with.
  - ○ You need to be in a position to demand this from others, and that demands that you are trustworthy.
    - If you have problems with your own integrity, you don't need to worry about anyone else; you and your organization have bigger issues.

On any given play, all eleven players on the field must be able to trust the players around them to do their jobs. Who is responsible for what assignment must be clearly defined, and the players must share honest and concise feedback with each other not only after every game, but also after every play. Eliminating individual agendas and misleading information is the only way the team can react and adjust to the ever-changing circumstances on the field, and then create a competitive advantage throughout the game.

- *Imagine the left guard failing to pick up a blitz because he was more interested in ensuring that "his man" didn't sack the quarterback.*

Flaw – Lack of integrity

- *What if certain members of the team lack the integrity to commit to the team winning the game and, instead, work only toward their own self-interests?*

The second-string running back noticed that the outside linebacker was cheating a step toward the sideline to help with containment because an ankle that he had turned in the first quarter was limiting his lateral movement, creating a large cutback lane. Between series, he slid over next to his good friend the Quarterback Coach, quietly pointed out the opportunity, and they agreed to keep it between the two of them until he was in the game.

Early in the fourth quarter the starter came off for a quick rest, and the Quarterback Coach bypassed the Offensive Coordinator and shared his insight directly with the Head Coach, who quickly relayed the information to the rest of the coaching staff. The play came off exactly as they anticipated, with the second-string back breaking the longest run of the game.

- *The running back hoped to exploit the situation into a starting assignment.*
- *The Quarterback Coach hoped that his insight would provide him with a shot at Offensive Coordinator.*
- *In an effort to promote themselves, they had failed to allow the team to take advantage of their competitor's weakness for the majority of the game.*
    - *By insisting that they receive the spotlight, they had intentionally worked against the primary goal of the team — winning the game.*

➢ While most fans would agree that the Quarterback Coach should be fired and the running back cut, this kind of manipulation has become so commonplace within many companies that it's barely even acknowledged.
  - It's impossible for this selfish approach to individual promotion to result in a positive working environment.
  - You cannot allow this type of behavior to take place in your business. It represents a breakdown of integrity, and

is only capable of limiting the potential of your company.
- Everyone must be working toward the same goal.

The night before the start of training camp, the Head Coach gathered the team together and gave the same speech that he always did to kick off every season. The team had to play as a team. The players had to communicate with each other. The coaches had to communicate with each other. The players and coaches had to communicate with each other. If there was a problem, he repeatedly emphasized that he didn't want to hear about it two weeks after the incident, or worse yet, read about it in the paper or learn about it from a television or radio broadcast. Although it may be a prerequisite of his job to address all of these concerns during the preseason speech, it's the least effective way he has of dealing with the issue. Integrity becomes the team philosophy only after:

- *The Head Coach and General Manager have a strong difference of opinion about the offensive scheme, but they debate their concerns with each other behind closed doors, not through the press.*
- *An assistant coach and a player get into an argument, and the player is pulled off the practice field and dealt with immediately.*
- *The first time O.T. throws up his hands in disgust because the ball wasn't thrown his direction, he is removed from the game and confronted.*
- *A piece of information that should have stayed within the team appears in the paper, and the next morning it's topic number one in the locker room before taking the practice field.*

The preseason speech may have been necessary, but like your company's mission statement, they are only words until they are consistently reinforced. It's naïve to assume that just because someone wrote or uttered some words that they represent reality. If they are not supported, not only do they become a meaningless policy, the coach will immediately, and deservedly, lose his credibility with the team.

- Do not fail to make transparency an absolute.
  - Integrity is where any organization, or for that matter any relationship, starts.
  - Make profit with integrity.
    - Your business cannot be successful without both.

KEY - Business 101

- It starts with making values an integral part of your business strategy when creating and maintaining long-term plans.
  - Emphasize integrity to your:
    - Employees
    - Customers
    - Suppliers
  - If you run into an individual or organization that can't be trusted, proceed with caution.
    - Business is too demanding, and evolving too quickly, to waste time dealing with people or organizations that aren't trustworthy.
- Another fatal mistake that I frequently encounter is the belief that integrity can be compartmentalized.

Facing the press, the team owner tries to rationalize signing O.T. "He may be unpredictable at practice and a nightmare in the locker room, but once he takes the field, he's all business."
They must be a team during practice. They must be a team in the locker room. They must be a team during the game. There is no such thing as being a great teammate part of the time.

  - My experience has repeatedly reinforced that people are not dishonest part of the time, or lacking character in only one area of their life. They may be better at concealing it in selected areas, but character is character, and honesty is honesty.

- You either are committed, or you aren't.
- Life shows all of us that good people make poor decisions, and it's part of the American way of life to give everyone a second chance.
    - The difference comes in how the individual reacts once they have made a mistake.
        - The person with character will step forward, own their mistake, and try to rectify the situation if possible.
        - The person of dubious character will move from one compromise to the next, always blaming some external source for their problems.
    - The same truth is undeniable for organizations, and the example starts at the top.
- Do not underestimate the commitment. It's easy to give a flowery speech or indiscriminately toss clever words into your mission statement.
    - Conversely, it's relentlessly demanding to consistently maintain integrity throughout any organization on an hour-by-hour, day-by-day basis.
    - It mandates that you deal with issues that compromise the integrity of the organization or the employees within.
    - It virtually guarantees that there will be times when you will be forced to:
        - Walk away from business.
        - Go through the pain of changing suppliers.
        - Part ways with employees who may even be friends.
- Mistakes can be corrected. We all make them.
- Decisions will prove wrong, and plans will require revision.
- Information will be incomplete, resulting in poor assumptions.

O.C.:   *"Our rookie running back struggled a bit more than I expected in week one. The first series he didn't read the blitz, and it led to a sack. During several running plays, he reverted back to his college habit of always looking for the big play rather than taking what the defense was giving him. Still, it isn't the rookie mistakes that bother me; that's just part of the painful process that we have been through many times with young players. I can teach him how to make better reads on the blitz and attack the line of scrimmage when there's nothing there. What I will not tolerate is him yelling at the offensive linemen on the sideline during games, or his lack of intensity during drills at practice."*

Head Coach: "*Sit him down and make our expectations clear. We have the same standards of behavior and effort from every player on this team. If he can't live up to that, assure him that there is a long list of players who would be willing take his spot on the roster.*"

- o A lack of integrity cannot be overcome — it can only be removed.
- ➢ If you have communicated your organization's commitment to character, and others chose another path, part ways.
  - o In the end, it's up to every individual to decide whether or not to be trustworthy.

O.T. makes comments during the post-game news conference that the quarterback is holding back the offense and a change may be necessary if they want to take advantage of his skills. That's the coward's way of dealing with the issue. If he truly believes that the quarterback is the problem, he needs to take it up with the quarterback and the coach behind closed doors. If the coach doesn't immediately take care of this situation, he will have a media circus on his hands, and the whole team will suffer. Entire seasons have fallen apart because this type of lack of integrity wasn't immediately addressed.

KEY – Be a professional

- ➢ Organizations collapse because this type of behavior is allowed to repeatedly take place unchallenged.
  - o The critical mistake that most companies make concerning integrity is that they take it for granted and fail to address issues.
  - o The conflict that it creates, more times than not, is healthy for the organization.
    - ▪ Honesty is only capable of exposing issues.
    - ▪ The lack of honesty is only capable of hiding the real issues that become more painful, and more expensive, the longer they are neglected.
  - o How can you make decisions without reality?
- ➢ Never assume that everyone is committed to integrity; after all, "it's in our mission statement," so it must be true.
  - o Reality check — no one, not even most of the employees in your own company, care about what your mission statement says.

What possible benefit could come from the Offensive Coordinator not providing the Head Coach with honest feedback? How could the team prepare for the next game? What if the Coordinator's favorite player was a poor running back? Would he pad his statistics and make sure to edit the game film so that only his friend's best runs were shown to the Head Coach?

KEY – Does this make sense?

- *Does that help the team win games?*
- *Does it make his friend a better running back?*

They need to either work with him to improve through honest feedback and development, or start handing the ball off to a more effective running back. It's no secret, probably not even to his friend, that a change would improve the team. Manipulating his statistics and editing the tape only hide the fact that his friend isn't doing the job; it doesn't change the reality that he is indeed producing unacceptable results.

KEY – Facts are stubborn things

Ignoring the facts slows down the process of solving the issue. For the team, this behavior is only capable contributing to losses. Players know when decisions aren't being made objectively. The Offensive Coordinator needs to have some faith in his friend that he can rise to the occasion and make a contribution.

- *Do what is best for the team.*

- ➢ Recently, a CEO, who was delivering quality results, was found to have taken some significant liberties on his resume.
    - o Now what? After all, CEOs are paid to deliver numbers, and he was very successful at that.
    - o Keep him, and you have established a very low integrity standard.
        - ▪ You have made it crystal clear that results are all that matter.
            - • Not only that, but results are rewarded regardless of the means utilized.
    - o You have just screamed your true ethics to your suppliers, customers, and employees, and have no right to complain when the next, even more egregious ethical boundary is violated.
    - o Send a message that everyone understands — fire him, period.

KEY – Be a professional

➤ Commit yourselves to doing the right thing.
  o Not the right thing for you, but the right thing for the organization.

Flaw – Ask how hard something is

  o This takes integrity.
➤ Another recent story repeating itself in the news has been the large number of companies that backdated options for many of their executives. The only rationale for this action is to increase the compensation for executives in a manner that has nothing to do with performance.
  o Ultimately, this is a real-life test for corporate boards across this country.
  o I keep reading that "it's a common practice."

That makes as much sense as a running back having a graduated bonus clause in his contract if he reaches a minimum of thousand yards, and then altering the starting point part way through the season to include the last two games of the previous year to ensure a maximum payout. Legitimizing unacceptable behavior doesn't suddenly make it honest behavior.

  o Backdating options is stealing regardless of how someone tries to rationalize it. There are people who should be going to prison.
    ▪ If you ever get an excuse that would be unacceptable from your eight-year-old, refuse to accept it from a professional.
      • Hold yourself and your organization to a higher standard.

81

The Head Coach must be able to trust the players to do their jobs. The players must be able to trust each other to do their jobs. This trust has to be based on proven actions, not just naive optimism. Everyone needs to be trustworthy. Winning the game must be the goal of every player and coach. When the team starts consistently winning games, the individual accolades will soon follow. The decisions that the Head Coach makes on a daily basis become much easier when everyone involved understands that integrity is an immovable object.

Chapter 9

Reviewing the Game Film
Insist on Accountability Every Day

Modern management has made accountability at the workplace a much more difficult and complex issue than it actually is. At the most fundamental level, accountability simply represents each of us doing what we are paid to do, and requiring that those employees we are responsible for are doing what they are paid to do. As managers, it carries the added perpetual responsibility of ensuring that the jobs your employees are performing are both clear to the individual and have a direct line to the objectives of the organization. You cannot replace this responsibility with an annual performance review comprised of a standard list of predetermined questions, or approach it as a necessary evil to be completed as quickly as possible and then filed away for another year. It must represent an ongoing process that results in a more valuable employee and company. It is an essential commitment that separates well-run organizations from the business just trying to survive another day.

➤ You can begin to insist on accountability only after you have committed to integrity as a non-negotiable position within your organization.

   o Every employee must be able to account for what he or she

is accomplishing, and specifically how it helps the organization.

- Why is this considered such a contentious position?
- Accomplishments are what we are all paid for.

o Regardless of what the latest psychobabble management program may claim, management needs to know what their employees are doing.

- How else can you continually review and adjust their actions to ensure that they are in line with the overall objectives of the organization?
  - You can't.

Flaw – Bad management

➢ Objectives and accomplishments of the individual must always be tied to the strategic goals of the organization.

o Additionally, objectives must always be specific, and their significance needs to be clearly understood by the person required to carry them out.

- That is the responsibility of management.
  - "Because I told you to" is never sufficient. Employees deserve to be kept informed.
- This is a great test for the legitimacy of actions and objectives. If you can't clearly explain their significance, making them a demand is unreasonable.
  - This is an essential exercise if you hope to reduce the "noise" within your company.

o Treat your employees like valuable, intelligent individuals.

- If they aren't, why are you paying them?

For defensive players, the objective is to get the offensive player with the ball on the ground as soon as possible. However, the noseguard's primary responsibility isn't necessarily to make a lot of tackles. If the

Defensive Coordinator's instructions are for him to mix it up with the offensive interior linemen, he will start randomly hitting the center or guard, eventually settling into a pattern of attacking the player who causes him the least amount of pain. With only that general guidance, it will become impossible to maximize his effectiveness because he doesn't understand how his objectives are tied to the rest of the defense, which remains focused on the ball carrier. He will begin to develop his own goals and strategies, which many times will fail to help achieve the overall objectives of the defense, but rather be geared toward what he feels is best. He may even develop habits that are counterproductive, all the while believing that he is doing a good job based on what he has been told.

Expanding on his original assignment to include how his role benefits the overall scheme of the defense, the noseguard's assignments will not only make more sense to him and improve his motivation, he can start making adjustments and providing feedback to the coaches that could benefit the effectiveness of the defense. Once he understands that clogging up the middle of the line of scrimmage is specifically designed to keep blockers off of the linebackers on running plays and make it more difficult for the other defensive linemen to be double teamed on passing plays, he can see how his role is integral to the success of every down. Now, instead of his job just being to hit the person across from him, his actions have been tied to the overall objectives of the defense, and he can take actions in the best interest of the team, rather than what he believes is best. Only after this clarification has been made can his position coach accurately begin to evaluate his effectiveness and work toward implementing improvements. Simply coming to the line of scrimmage and hitting someone hard is no longer the job description. He now can see why his role is essential to the success of the defense, even if his contribution is rarely measurable in the statistics.

> ➢ As a manager, it's essential that you direct employees to concentrate on tasks that are in line with the objectives of the organization.
>> o If you lose this focus, your employees wind up doing "stuff." They will work on what appears to be important or, even more commonly, what feels critical at that moment.

- o Without constantly refocusing, by default, managers will fall into a pattern of merely keeping employees busy.
  - An employee can work hard, fulfill goals that they believe are important, and still fail to create value.

KEY - Business 101

- ➤ Once clear, fair objectives have been established, every employee is then responsible for doing his or her job well.
  - o If they can't, or choose not to, you have a situation that must be addressed.
    - You must go back, determine why, and fix the problem.

"Sorry I missed that block. I guess I wasn't paying attention last week at practice when we made the changes to that play. By the way, when will you be out of the hospital?"

- ➤ Accountability must permeate the organization.
  - o Everyone must be held to the same high standard of accountability.
  - o You must hold yourself to a high standard of accountability.
    - It *always* starts with you.
  - o Never ignore that you cannot pass on high expectations to others until you have demanded the same high expectations for yourself.

KEY – Be a professional

At the snap of the ball, the fullback recognized that the right flat was being vacated by the outside linebacker and, based on his years of experience, knew that he would be able to slide out of the backfield and be wide open for a pass. Unfortunately, the play called wasn't a pass play; it was a sweep to the right, and the fullback's primary responsibility was to pick up the outside linebacker to create a running lane. With the rest of the offense running a different play, predictably, the call resulted in a five-yard loss.

In the fullback's mind, he had done everything correctly because the Offensive Coordinator had been too busy to include him in the play call. He had been left to carry out his assignment based on his years of experience, rather than in a coordinated effort with the rest of the offense. The fact that he was wide open on the play only reinforced his decision, and led him to complain about the competency of both the quarterback and coach after the game in the locker room to some of his teammates and the press. As they left the stadium, the Offensive Coordinator and the Head Coach had a quick discussion of their own, concerning if they needed to consider replacing the fullback in the lineup. Despite the obvious breakdown of the play, they continued to fail to address the real shortfall of not openly and honestly communicating, which can only lead to more frustratingly poor results, regardless of who is lined up at fullback.

> - You must continually review individual objectives in context of the overall goals of the organization.
>   - As organizational goals change, you cannot assume that individual objectives will remain the same, or that employees are even aware of all of the changes.
>   - They will only be aware if you communicate the changes.
> - Insist on working with those who hold themselves accountable and are capable of accomplishing objectives.
>   - This single uncompromising philosophy of demanding accountability will do more to drive an organization forward than any new program you can implement.
> - Before trying to roll out some management philosophy that promises to change the mind-set of the organization, adopt the most basic of all criteria:
>   - Make sure that every job makes sense.

o Make sure that everyone understands, and is capable of, performing his or her responsibilities.
o Once in place, make sure everyone is performing his or her job.
  ▪ Warning — this is a constant way of life, not a fad. Consistency and fairness are prerequisites to success.
o If you are not committed on a daily basis, your employees will quickly sense that you don't take accountability seriously, and the result will be that you destroy your credibility.
  ▪ Once it's gone, getting it back can prove impossible.
o There is a good reason why employees don't take new company initiatives and philosophies seriously.
  ▪ Management is rarely committed, and it's easy to see when something does not have honest support; they fail to hold themselves to the same standard.

Flaw – Lack of integrity

o Accountability is hard work and demands commitment.
➤ Holding an organization accountable requires that you constantly:
  o Provide specific direction.
  o Measure accomplishments.
  o Reevaluate objectives for relevancy.
  o Refocus as the world around you adapts and changes.
  o Help others to attain their goals.
    ▪ Build credibility.
  o Follow up on progress.
  o Start over again.

There are four receivers battling for the final spot on the roster. If he is committed to winning games, the Head Coach must keep the players at every position that gives them the best opportunity to win. There is no room for favoritism. The coach needs to provide all of the players with the playbook and the proper instruction. He has to make sure that they all receive sufficient reps during practice to develop their skills. Throughout the preseason, he must put them on the field in critical situations so that he has the opportunity to evaluate their performance under the real-time pressure of the game. Finally, he has to meet with the position coach for feedback and then, based on the evidence that the players have provided through their efforts, objectively make the decision. Once the decision is made, he has to:

- *Support them.*
- *Demand that they perform.*

➢ Keep the bar high for everyone.
   o You never help someone by keeping expectations artificially low. Set attainable goals, but make sure that they meet the needs of the organization.
   o Show some faith in those around you.
      ▪ Support them at every possible opportunity.
   o Have faith in yourself.
   o Seek support from others, and never stop learning.

Although it may be an essential part of the overall process, it's not enough for the coaching staff to sit down at the end of the year to discuss and evaluate the players on the team. Throughout the season, every play is analyzed to determine the effectiveness of all eleven players on the field. Physical and mental mistakes are addressed; practices are refocused to improve areas of weaknesses. Discussions go late into the night regarding what changes need to be made, how game plans can be strengthened, and where individual players need upgrading or support. Players are held accountable for their performances and specifically shown where and why improvements are essential. Position coaches are held accountable for their area of responsibility. The Head Coach is held responsible for the team's shortfalls. Every individual is held accountable not just for the success or failure of the season, but the success or failure of every game, and the success or failure of every play. In the end, even for that one team that can claim the title of World Champions, the bar is raised another notch, because as soon as the celebration is over, there is another season to prepare for.

Chapter 10

Play the Opponent
Dealing with Emerging Markets

The business landscape has shifted so rapidly over recent years that many companies were caught completely unprepared to deal with the changes. There is no denying that the inability to adapt forced many well-known companies out of business, depressed the margins of entire markets, and has left many others with uncertain futures. In a very short period of time, skills and industries that were once considered to have unquestioned security have faltered, or even disappeared. Simultaneously, other companies have thrived in the global marketplace and remain well positioned for continued success as circumstances evolve. Although there are undeniably innumerable structural and market forces influencing the continued viability of any business, I consistently find that successful companies posture themselves to always be prepared to make the rapid adjustments necessary to exploit market transitions as they develop. Their leadership not only refuses to be overwhelmed by the pace of change, they embrace it.

Change isn't treated as if it was a unique event; it's integral to their organization. Instead of wasting time reminiscing about the past or complaining about how unfair the competition has become, they focus on addressing the challenges. These managers recognize that although they may not have any control over global economic developments, they do have total control over how they react to them, and recognize that they are responsible for their reactions. They focus on the opportunities created, deal with the threats, and refuse to waste energy discussing the negative aspects of change. Throughout the storm, they remain professional.

- ➢ Rather than dissecting the infinite amount of available statistical detail and then attempting to present an in-depth analysis regarding emerging markets, I believe that it would be far more beneficial to devote a few short pages to a sampling of high-level trends regarding global changes.
  - o The objective is to present a cross-section of data that, although far from all-encompassing, will make you realize that you must take the initiative to become constantly aware of the specific global developments within your business that will influence the future.
  - o The United Nations' population estimates reveal how the landscape of business will be irrevocably changed.
    - All projections are based on United Nations' figures. Visit www.un.org for the most current information.
- ➢ Considering that in the past the global economy for most western companies ignored much of the globe, I will start by just highlighting the current populations in the areas where the majority of their business took place:
  - o United States — 300 million.
  - o Western Europe — 400 million.
    - For many companies, this is the only part of Europe that they recognized. Going forward, indeed today, that is an outdated presupposition.
  - o Europe: total population — 728 million.
  - o Japan — 127 million.
- ➢ The world unfolding before you will be very different from the past. It remains a gross oversimplification to examine only a few countries; however, as the next logical step, compare the following figures with the populations of the two most visible, and obsessed over, entrants into the global economy:

- o China — 1.3 billion.
- o India — 1.1 billion.
  - There is a legitimate academic argument that these figures don't accurately reflect the current increase of participants in the global economy because not all of their populations are currently engaged. However, you must consider their impact over the past decade, and recognize their intention to include an increasingly greater percentage of their populations as their economies expand. This will not only ensure that the rate of change we have experienced will continue, if not accelerate, but their inclusion will result in continued pressure on many segments of traditional economies as markets struggle to absorb the new markets and competitors.
- ➤ Because you must focus your attention forward rather than backward, even more significant than the population in these emerging economies are their rates of growth and demographic changes. Estimates at the top line for 2025, which is coming much more rapidly than any of us would care to admit, reveal that a dramatic transformation is virtually guaranteed:
  - o United States — 350 million; a 50-million increase.
  - o Europe total — 707 million; a 21-million ***decrease.***
    - This trend will accelerate as Europe loses an additional 54 million residents by 2050.
      - Everything you know about European demographics is about to become obsolete.
  - o Japan — 125 million; a two-million ***decrease.***
  - o China — 1.4 billion; a 200-million increase.
    - Current projections are that the Chinese population will level off at this approximate level.
  - o India — 1.4 billion; a 300-million increase.
    - Note that India will be increasing in number by approximately the current population of the United States over less than two decades.
- ➤ It's also becoming increasingly obvious that just because we have

historically ignored many regions, some newcomers will undoubtedly command an increasingly significant position in the future:

- o Latin America/Caribbean — 697 million; a 136-million increase.
- o Africa — 1.3 billion; a 438-million increase.
  - This gain represents nearly 150% of the current U.S. population.
  - Lumping the African continent into a single set of market and cultural assumptions is a dangerous, and incorrect, position. Large parts of this often-ignored continent will develop into global players in the near future.

➤ Your old assumptions are no longer relevant in today's business world.
➤ Your current assumptions won't be relevant in the business world of the future.

KEY – Facts are stubborn things

- o ***Think*** about the changes and what they will mean to you:
  - Threats — the most sweeping in history if you are unprepared.
  - Opportunities — the greatest in history if you are prepared.

➤ In less than twenty years, the world will add over 1.4 billion people.
  - o That represents adding 4½ United States to the global population.
    - What will be the effect on:
      - Employment trends?
      - Housing?
      - Energy consumption?
      - Pharmaceuticals?
      - Communications?
      - Your current products and services?

- o Are you ready?
- ➤ What do these changes specifically mean to the traditional economic powers?
    - o As the global percentage of the United States' population decreases, and new economies around the world continue to gather momentum, it's likely that our economic influence will decrease accordingly.
        - In 1950, the United States represented six percent of the global population.
        - Currently, the figure stands at five percent.
        - By 2025, we will have stabilized between four and five percent of global totals.
    - o European influence will evolve even more dramatically over the same period:
        - In 1950, twenty-two percent of the global population was in Europe.
        - Currently, that number has been cut in half to eleven percent.
        - By 2025, less than nine percent of the population will be in Europe.
        - By 2050, that number will be at seven percent, less than a third of the 1950 level.
    - o You, and your business, must think in global terms.
- ➤ In addition to the population shift toward developing economies, the transformations taking place within traditional economies will revolutionize many businesses:
    - o Globally, there were 131 million people over 65 in 1950.
    - o By 2050, there will be 1.4 billion over 65 years of age.
        - In the United States alone there will be 79 million people over the age of 65 by 2050.
            - There will be 21 million over the age of 85!
        - Western Europe is facing the staggering challenge of having nearly 50% of their population over 65 by the year 2050.
            - What changes in the market will all of this bring?

- Consider the new opportunities that will emerge just from these developments. Enormous new markets will naturally surface, and someone will fill the needs.
- ➢ China has become an obsession.
- ➢ India has become an obsession.
  - o Outsourcing has become an increasingly real threat to many organizations and individuals, and if you focus only on the politicians and media, we are all doomed, and only they can rescue us.
    - ▪ Unquestionably, emerging markets are forever altering the face of business for many companies, and will continue to do so.
  - o Politicians have taken advantage of people's fears in an effort to translate them into votes — that's what they do.
  - o The media has used sensationalism to sell their products — that's what they do.
    - ▪ Note — in both cases, honestly communicating the positive and negative realities of these changes isn't necessarily in their best interests.
      - In many cases, objectivity actually runs counterproductive to their goals.
  - o History has repeatedly demonstrated that manual labor follows low costs. One of the fundamental developments taking place currently is that white-collar employees are no longer exempt from the process.
    - ▪ Many managers who have self-righteously proclaimed that they aren't responsible for blue-collar jobs shifting overseas because the global economy ultimately determines compensation suddenly have become much more protectionist as their paychecks are threatened.
- ➢ Stop obsessing about China and India, and start to think.
  - o Too many companies are so caught up in self-pity that they are ignoring:

KEY – Be a professional

Unfortunately, no team has the luxury of selecting the opponent that they would prefer to play from week to week. They aren't allowed to schedule only the teams with losing records or injury-ravaged lineups. They have to play the next team on the schedule. The defending Super Bowl champions boasting a 12-0 record are rolling into town, and the buzz among the television analysts and radio talk show listeners is of a perfect season. Their offense is on track to lead the league, and their defense is threatening to establish a new record for the fewest yards ever allowed per game. So, what do they do now, not show up for the game? How about if the team stops practicing and calls a meeting to discuss how unbeatable they are? That would be a ridiculous, and irresponsible, game plan. A plan, or lack thereof, guaranteed to lose.

Flaw – Ask how hard something is

➢ Evaluating new markets and developing new areas of strength that your company can exploit must become a way of life.
  o You must get to know your markets and competition.

The team would double their efforts, adjust, train, examine every detail, and then take the field and play the game with as much intensity as possible. The key being that the team would take the field and play the game to the best of their ability.

KEY – Be a professional

➢ Don't for a moment underestimate the emerging threats; the global economy has and will continue to result in fundamental market changes that will permanently affect most organizations.
  o You simply need to change the way you look at it.

- China and India are not the issue, and never will be.
  o The issue is the market, its opportunities and threats.

KEY - Business 101

o Return to business fundamentals and objectively evaluate your company's future:
- Are emerging markets going to create additional competitors?
- Is their emergence going to result in potential new markets?

➤ Examine China, India, and any other emerging market in the same manner that you would any other opportunity or threat. Put the emotion aside.
  o Are their cost structures a threat to you?
- If so, what is your plan?
  o Are their locations a threat to you?
- If so, what is your plan?
  o Do they represent a potential market for you?
- If so, what is your plan?
  o Are your products and services even relevant in the future?
- If not, what is your plan?

In a single series, the team's entire season was jeopardized when both their noseguard and middle linebacker went down with injuries. At both positions, the backups are rookies with almost no game experience. To make matters worse, they have to travel to the team leading the league in rushing next Sunday.

D.C.:   *"I hate to state the obvious, but there is no way that we are going to be able to stop their running game. We're just going to have to hope that our offense can put a lot of points on the board."*

No head coach would allow this response from the Defensive Coordinator. It's his job to develop the best possible solution. Injuries are an unfortunate reality of the game, not an excuse to fail.

- *The rookie replacements are going to need extra time in both the film room and on the practice field.*
- *The roster needs to be evaluated to determine if there is anyone else who can move over and provide the team a better opportunity for success.*
- *The General Manager needs to get on the phones and scour the waiver wires for experienced players who could provide support.*

Regardless of how good of a running game the other team has, or how depleted their roster might be, the objective for the team hasn't changed. They have to win the game, and an essential element of the strategy is doing everything possible to limit their running yards.

> Stop getting the "deer in the headlights" look.
> - Think about what changes mean to your organization, and take appropriate action.
>   - You aren't going to be allowed to take your ball and go home just because the competition just acquired the biggest, fastest players and permanently changed the dynamics of the game.
> Never rely on someone else to bail you out of your problems.
> - Politics may be a reality in global business; however, you must always assume that you are going to participate in a free market.
>   - It's a mistake to believe that the same politicians who routinely screw up global trade agreements will magically fix them.
> - You must take advantage of free markets. By definition, they create both threats and opportunities.

G.M.:   *"Coach, I watched the film, and there is no getting around the fact that they are too fast for us to handle.*

After considering all of the options, I petitioned the league to mandate that their backs and receivers wear five-pound ankle weights for the next two seasons until we can draft some faster players."

➤ Panicking, overreacting, and praying that someone bails you out are not legitimate strategic plans.

Flaw – Bad management

o Companies that are obsessing about the global economy have replaced professional management with reactionary management. As a result, they are losing precious time that should be invested into addressing the challenges ahead.
o These are the largest new markets in the history of mankind; you *cannot have that potential without also having significant and formidable competition enter the marketplace.*
  ▪ There were a lot of politicians who were either ignorant of rudimentary economic fundamentals or closed their eyes and pretended this wasn't the case, ignoring, as they frequently do:

KEY – Facts are stubborn things

  ▪ That is how free markets are designed to work.
o And, as in this case, the threats typically precede the opportunities for the more developed economies.
  ▪ Sorry, that is life in the global marketplace.
  ▪ It's the unavoidable reality of future business.
    • Get over it.

100

KEY – Be a professional

➤ If running a successful business were a simple endeavor, everyone you know would be a millionaire working at his or her leisure.
   o It's not easy, and it is going to become increasingly more challenging.
      ▪ Stop assuming that your company cannot compete.
   o Have some faith in yourself and your organization. Get to work and rise to the occasion.

Up and down the roster, they have spent years building their team for speed. The home turf is fast, and the weather conditions always ideal in the dome. Now, all because a referee blew a call in week three that cost them home field advantage throughout the playoffs, they have to go on the road and play the Divisional Championship in Chicago, and the forecasters are calling for heavy snow and high winds. All week there has been an unrelenting stream of media discussion concerning how instant replay failed, and their team is now unfairly faced with playing a game in the worst of possible conditions. The Head Coach has two choices:

- *Complain to the league, his players, and the press, lamenting that home field advantage was clearly robbed from his team.*
- *Conversely, spend his time and energy preparing the team for the reality that the game will in fact be played in Chicago, in the snow and wind.*
   o *Which alternative will give his team the greatest opportunity for success?*

Chapter 11

Preparing to Win
Working in the Real World

The more that you obsess over the growing tide of global threats to your career and business, the greater the vacuum of anxiety created for those with the next feel-good piece of enlightenment to fill. There is an increasing desire to embrace philosophies that are flawed at their very core because they seek to address very complex issues with simple solutions based on little more than feelings. Our society has enjoyed a technological and economic advantage that has resulted in our enjoying the highest standard of living in history, and we would all like to believe that we could sustain this edge indefinitely. It seems to make perfect sense that if we can just safeguard this perceived advantage, businesses can thrive, and our standard of living can be maintained or even improved.

The underlying problem with this belief is that it is overly simpleminded, and likely to create a level of complacency that will ensure that our standard of living deteriorates. You are not inherently smarter than the rest of the planet simply by having had the good fortune of being born in a developed country. Although many of our schools continue to produce high-quality students, test scores have repeatedly demonstrated that our educational system as a whole is not keeping pace with much of the world. In math and science, the United States now ranks eighteenth out of the twenty-four countries surveyed. The Chinese are currently graduating significantly more engineers than we are, and depending on what source you choose to believe, the Indians are graduating as many or more. Nearly fifty percent of the patents issued *__in this country__* don't originate here. These facts aren't necessarily good or bad within themselves, but they do represent a new reality that isn't going to disappear just because segments of the population are uncomfortable with it. The past economic success of this country cannot be treated as a birthright that future generations are automatically entitled to. Quite to the contrary, history would teach us that the vanity of dominant cultures has always preceded their decline.

As an individual, the future is going to demand that you commit to the lifelong process of challenging yourself through education and initiative. As a company, you must cultivate a culture that relentlessly pursues learning and productivity. As a society, we are well past the point of debate; it is vital that we commit to developing the means to provide a world-class education to everyone with the ambition to pursue one. The ability to out-think the competition is not something achieved by decree; it can only be earned through effort. Individuals must be prepared to give an honest effort every day. Companies must treat their employees fairly. Imaginative feel-good sayings won't alter the reality that we cannot commit to anything less.

- ➢ Work smarter, not harder
  - o One of the great sayings in business. Alas, if it were only that simple.

Flaw – Management by fuzzy feeling

- o Slick-sounding or overly appealing messages are rarely anything but slick-sounding, overly appealing messages.
  - ▪ Those who would prefer not to work harder almost always espouse this philosophy.

103

Flaw – Lack of integrity

- There is also the unspoken implication that the person enlightening you has no need to work harder, because they are already so much smarter than the rest of us.
  - Taken further, they would prefer not to work smarter, either. The fluffy message encompasses the whole of their intellectual contribution.
- Let's be honest; sayings like this make us feel better about an increasingly uncertain future.
  - For at least a moment, everyone can live in denial about globalization threatening their business, new competition taking market share, eroding margins, rising costs, and nagging personnel issues.
    - In short, the real issues of managing a business.
    - The hard business realities impatiently waiting for you every morning.
- You simply plug in the fuzzy saying and go to lunch on the company credit card.

KEY – Never get too comfortable

Head Coach: *"By now I'm sure that you have all watched the tapes and are well aware of what their defense is capable of. The last time that we played them, we barely had two hundred yards of offense, not to mention that we were thoroughly beaten up and lost two starters for the season. All of this considered, does anyone have any meaningful input before we start to develop our offensive game plan?"*

O.C.: *"I added several new wrinkles that they haven't seen before, and changed up some of the blocking assignments to try and minimize the physical abuse."*

Head Coach: *"That's a start, but we can't assume that disguising plays and altering blocking assignments will be enough to produce sufficient offense. We cannot win unless we find a way to put more points on the board, and we cannot do that without gaining some control over the line of scrimmage."*

> ➤ Back to reality:
>> o Yes, part of the saying is true — you need to work smarter.
>>> ▪ However, at the risk of being the bearer of bad news, you also need to out-work the competition.

KEY – Facts are stubborn things

> o You must embrace the philosophy that you are committed to excellence in every aspect of your business.
>> ▪ Although it may be difficult to ultimately succeed in every facet, you cannot acquiesce any critical element just because it's difficult.

Flaw – Ask how hard something is

The team that won the division last year overpowered most of their opponents because of a revolutionary strength-training program that they had developed in the off-season, which resulted in giving them a significant advantage at the point of attack. After reviewing hours of tape in the off-season, the Offensive Coordinator has come to the conclusion that he must dedicate himself to ensuring that his team has a better understanding of the offensive scheme than any other team in the league. That is the only hope he sees to overcome the obvious strength disparity.

KEY – Does this make sense?

The Offensive Coordinator's decision makes absolutely no sense because he is failing to address the team's well-established strength liability. Increasing the understanding of the offensive scheme may be a legitimate objective separately, and could even help to create a competitive advantage; however, it isn't an excuse for ignoring the reality that the team must get stronger if they are going to successfully compete. In a game that is physical in nature, strength is an imperative fundamental, and they cannot allow the deficiency to continue. The objective must be not only to close the gap, but also to work toward creating a strength advantage.

KEY – Facts are stubborn things

It is an undeniable fact of winning football games that the team cannot simply allow the opposition to control the line of scrimmage. If they want to win, the coaching staff needs to consider all aspects of the game. They must:

- *Out-work them.*
- *Out-think them.*
- *Develop better game plans.*
- *Develop better coaching strategies.*
- *Draft and develop better players, etc.*

KEY – Be a professional

Long-term success depends on developing and maintaining all of these strengths. By default, not addressing all aspects of the game limits the effectiveness of the team, and winning games will become increasingly more difficult. Assuming that continuous improvement in only certain areas of the organization will lead to victories is denying the evolution of the game and its increasing competitiveness. They are replacing total commitment to their team's success with a dependence on the competition to adopt a similar, limited approach to the game.

- Anything less is a complete denial of the constantly evolving landscape of business and globalization. Have you looked closely at the world unfolding all around you?
  - The inclusion of China, India, and Eastern Europe into the market has made obsolete old assumptions.
    - As detailed in chapter ten, literally billions of people have been added to the labor pool in recent years, and this includes many professions that have historically been exempt from low-cost alternatives.
    - A lot of managers need to stop pretending that they can skate through their careers, earning a good living by maintaining historical levels of commitment and effort.
      - Everything has changed; you must take the responsibility and initiative to adapt.
  - What is the one common objective these companies and workers in emerging economies want?
    - They want what you have.
      - They represent billions of potential competitors around the globe who are willing to put in the effort, pursue the education, and develop the strategic plans to be successful.

107

o It's cavalier to think that you can get away with any less and be successful.

Flaw – Bad management

➢ Welcome to the new world; stop whining and get accustomed to it.
  o You cannot afford to waste any time or effort reminiscing about how business was done in the past — it doesn't matter.

Flaw – Debating if change is good or bad

➢ You need to out-work, and out-think, the competition if you want to succeed.
  o And you can succeed. It's not just about all of the threats to our standard of living.
    ▪ The world has never offered more opportunities.
    ▪ The billions of potential competitors also represent billions of potential customers.

Unrelenting competition is why the professional football player invests long hours in the weight room, studies film to try and create even the slightest advantage, and then practices the subtlest of techniques until they become reflex. Every player is constantly aware that there is a long line of prospects willing to do whatever is necessary to improve, with the single-minded objective of taking his job. The financial rewards of playing at the professional level create enormous incentives that result in intense competition for every roster position.

For the team, consider playing smarter, but failing to invest the necessary time at the weight room. They might become experts at anticipating what the other team is going to do based on tendencies picked up through hours of film study, but they will fail to be successful if the other team is physically better prepared and establishes control throughout the game. However, if they do all of the strength training, but ignore the intellectual aspects of the game, they may be in a better position to dominate the line of scrimmage, but without the ability to understand the tendencies of their opponent, their strengths will never be as effective as they could potentially be. The team committed to both disciplines has a competitive advantage that is very difficult to overcome by any opponent who limits their areas of commitment.

- *If they want to win the game, and it is their job to win, they need to be the best in both the weight room and the film room.*
- *There are no substitutes committing to both out-working and out-thinking the competition.*
- *There are no short cuts or clever sayings that will make them feel better about their game plan or magically result in an alternate reality that makes the next game less demanding.*

Flaw – Management by fuzzy feeling

It starts with the Head Coach demanding excellence from himself, everyone involved with the team, and not accepting excuses for any lack of preparation. Only the players willing to make this commitment are worth investing the coaching staff's time in training and developing. Talent alone is not enough. Preparation isn't enough. The team must have both.

Chapter **12**

<u>The Players Decide the Game</u>
Drowning in Systems

here must be an easy answer for the challenges that we all face on a daily basis, right? If you can just drill down to the root cause of the problem, enlightened management teaches us that we can make improvements without any nasty personal confrontations. You can add work instructions, additional training, or form focus groups that will eliminate the organization's deficiencies, all the while making everyone feel better about themselves and the company. You can get the staff to acknowledge that problems are never the fault of well-meaning employees, unless of course you are an employee who happens to be in upper management, in which case, it is all your fault.

I have never worked with a company that didn't wholeheartedly proclaim that their people were their greatest asset. It has developed into such a reflex reply that I can count on management to not only regurgitate the exact same philosophy regardless of the organization, but deliver it with the same inflection points and tone of seriousness. If their commitment is as genuine and they labor so hard to make you believe, then clearly demonstrable evidence that they are investing more time developing employees, as opposed to developing the systems that their employees work in, should be readily available. However, despite the sincerity of management's initial proclamation, if you request such evidence, you are likely to be buried under mission statements, value statements, fancy focus-group nonsensical statements, or even personnel policies primarily designed to reduce the company's legal exposure, rather than actual evidence. Never make the mistake of confusing the implementation of systems, and formulation of official words, with developing individuals. If you don't have evidence supporting your commitment, the commitment isn't real, and it's about time that you realized that every employee in your organization already knows it.

- In the interest of full disclosure, it's only fair to start this chapter with a disclaimer: the unrelenting devotion to management systems is a major stress point for me.
  - Even more distressing, the lack of any substantive debate about management systems resulted in a longer, more detailed chapter than I would have preferred.
- Becoming a system-dominated organization has somehow evolved into the normal course of business in our culture, and this is increasingly suffocating many companies because their rationality is considered beyond reproach, and as a result, they are rarely honestly challenged.
  - It's not that there is anything inherently wrong with systems. Disciplines within any company are essential. The issue is the way that they are implemented or, better put, shoved down the throat of an organization and its employees.
    - Honestly, how many of the systems in your company benefit the business?
      - More succinctly, how many *increase* profitability?

KEY - Business 101

- How many companies become so consumed by

their systems that they eventually drown in them?
- More succinctly, how many *decrease* profitability?
  o Left unchecked, systems take on a life of their own, becoming the monster that self-perpetuates itself through the mentality that if you challenge any part of the system, you are out of touch with modern managerial advancements, and therefore, your opinion is irrelevant.
    ▪ Arrogance and incompetence in equal measure.

Flaw – Bad management

➢ Be fair. Think. Your task, your obligation, is to make a profit by offering a product or service. Any systems implemented by the organization are only beneficial as they contribute toward that means.
  o Anything less is just another cost; everything else is just a cost.
  o Every asset, of which time is a key element, must be subjected to this litmus test. If you aren't willing to do this, ask yourself, why?

From the beginning of training camp to the final day of the season, every meeting, every practice drill, every stretching regimen is designed with a single purpose — to prepare the team to win. As the coaching staff reviews the week ahead, they are constantly searching for more effective ways to improve their preparation and eliminate routines that don't contribute toward their objectives. They would never consider including a drill that resulted in reinforcing poor fundamentals or allowed players to avoid personal responsibility.

➢ The danger with any system-dominated company is that the system becomes more of a focal point within the business than the actual business.

- o More precisely, any system becomes ***destructive*** when it becomes primarily what employees do. A business is not its systems any more than a team is its playbook.
  - ▪ Left unchecked, some of the better-known systems more closely resemble a religion than a business tool.
- o Your customer has it; therefore, you must have it too. It validates ***their*** decision.
  - ▪ "We did it, so it must be a brilliant business strategy."
  - ▪ "Not only that, but if you don't have it, you must not be a real company. After all, we have it, and if you don't get it, we will outsource your business to India or China."
    - • "Which we may do anyway. By the way, we demand a cost down."
- o The problem is, when management abdicates their responsibilities, systems beget systems, and the same thought process that starts with the best of intentions to improve the company winds up strangling it.
  - ▪ The organization develops a systems mentality, where the system mandates that the answer to every issue is the development of more systems.

The Offensive Line Coach committed his entire off-season into developing the most exhaustive program for improving the performance of linemen that had ever been assembled. His five- volume, 1,237-page system was not only the most comprehensive approach; it contained a self-monitoring mechanism to address any areas of weakness within the program and then permanently build all upgrades into the process.

Initially, he had set out to assemble an outline that detailed every aspect of training; however, it had taken on a life of its own, once he began his research, and now encompassed the players' entire day. Book One, based on an analysis of a three- day comprehensive physical exam by a battery of medical professionals, resulted in individualized breakfast, lunch, dinner, and supplementary diet schedules for every day of the week.

Book Two, the smallest of the volumes at 129 pages, was packed full of diagrams to teach proper stretching and yoga techniques, and included a CD to ensure that only correct methods were being followed. Each book could be customized for the demands of the individual player based on their position and needs, and included a weekly schedule for face-to-face meetings with certified trainers.

Book Three focused on weight training and brought together the most innovative experts in the field. The coach was convinced that the improved results would eventually overcome the ill feelings that were bound to develop when the team's strength coach realized that he had been bypassed. Like the stretching and yoga book, this volume was filled with numerous sketches and an accompanying CD.

Book Four, which focused on film study techniques, had turned out to be much longer and more detailed than originally expected. Once he began to delve into documenting proper disciplines, it had become obvious to him that the level of detail would be extreme and, as an intellectual exercise, was going to mandate continuous testing. As a result, the first half of the book dealt with the specifics of leaning proper film-watching techniques, and the second half represented a certification process that every offensive lineman would need to pass before they would be allowed to check out their helmet. The certification could be continually upgraded to ensure that they were following "best in class" techniques.

The final book focused on skills to be reinforced during practice. By requiring each player to have a verifiable understanding of all 437 drills, they could be confident of instinctively reacting to any situation that presented itself during a game. The accompanying four-CD set demonstrated every drill in detail and included an interactive simulation program so that the players could run through any practice that they might have missed.

The beauty of the system was that each player would be issued their own laptop where they would enter data after every event throughout their day. With the wireless coverage in the area, the coach could be constantly updated on their progress, complete with detailed charts and trend lines for every player. With training camp less than a week off, he had presented his plan to the Offensive Coordinator that morning, who had pointed out that his system left no time for the players to sleep, which the Line Coach quietly noted could be the basis for volume six. The Offensive Coordinator had also sarcastically noted that data entry would consume the majority of the player's day, leaving little time to actually practice, and that they would need to add staff to manage all of the information. The Offensive Line Coach was also still fuming about his parting criticism that possibly he should consider evaluating the linemen based on their ability to block the player across from them. It was just that kind of limited vision that had him considering departing for a new team at the conclusion of the season.

> ➤ Another stumbling block that companies encounter is that the words sound so good and, at least on the surface, make so much sense.
>> o They tend to be so warm and comforting, which should always be one of your clearest warning signs that something is a potential trap.

Flaw – Management by fuzzy feeling

> ➤ One of the most common fuzzy warning signs you will encounter is the proclamation of auditing the system, not the people.
>> o It sounds so benign, so safe.

It's third and fourteen, and the team desperately needs a big play. The slot receiver runs straight up the field twenty yards and cuts outside, leaving plenty of room to work back to the ball and still get the first down. The offensive line digs in and holds off the oncoming rush, creating a clear passing lane. The quarterback takes his drop, steps up into the pocket, and fires the ball to the sideline just inside the first-down marker. Fundamentally, everything is executed to perfection. However, there seems to be a problem. The receiver is still in his break as the ball goes sailing harmlessly into the opposing bench. Fourth down, bring on the punt unit.

The systems-dominated team immediately calls an emergency

meeting, and a focus group with players from a variety of positions is assembled along the sideline. They initiate a brainstorming session to break down the play and develop potential patches. They need to put work instructions in place to make sure that the same problem doesn't surface again the next time they call the play. Once everyone is comfortable with the initial recommendations, the scribe writes them on the board for the group to review. After much discussion, they agree to have the quarterback hold the ball for an extra second to allow for the receiver to make his break. The paperwork is initiated, all of the members of the focus group sign off on the change, and then congratulate each other on a successful resolution.

Later in the game, a similar situation presents itself. With the fix in place, they confidently call the same play, assured of a successful outcome. The quarterback holds the ball for an extra second precisely as the new work instructions spelled out. The receiver gets out of his break and looks back just in time to see his quarterback get swarmed under by the defensive end. Unfortunately, the same extra second that allowed for the receiver to complete his route was the same extra second the opponent's all-pro defensive end needed to reach the quarterback. The only thing different about bringing out the punt team after this series is that they have to wait for an extra two minutes while the trainer helps their dazed quarterback back to the bench.

This time, the focus group comes to a quick consensus that the offensive line needs to hold off the rush for an additional second. Considering that their conference leads the league in sacks, it's also thought prudent to assemble a secondary problem-solving team that will make recommendations on optimal blocking techniques, weight lifting diagrams, and proper diet for maximum performance. Problem solved, congratulate everyone involved.

KEY – Does this make sense?

Two weeks later, they are faced with third and fourteen, and call on their favorite play, which by now has become several pages longer in the

116

playbook, as well as the subject of an off-site team meeting. Much to their delight, the line holds, the quarterback takes advantage of the extra second to deliver a strike, yet this time the cornerback easily steps in front of the receiver and intercepts the ball, returning it thirty-five yards for a touchdown. For all of their additional work instructions, the result of the play is deteriorating with each successive time that it's called. The Offensive Coordinator decides that it's time to bring in the Head Coach to the meeting.

> ➤ Does any of this sound eerily familiar?

After a few minutes of polite debate over what went wrong with the two previous focus groups, the Receiver's Coach finally stands up.

Rec. Coach: *"I think that I know precisely what the root cause is."* This better be good, because he isn't following the company-wide meeting protocol that every coach, including himself, signed off on. *"Our slot receiver runs a 5.9-second forty-yard dash. He's so slow that it forces our line to block longer than is realistic, exposes our quarterback to unnecessary hits, and is far too easy for a professional cornerback to cover even if we do run the play to perfection."*

> ➤ Time to audit the player and the system.
> - o The play was well designed.
> - o The offensive line did their jobs.
> - o The quarterback did his job.

KEY – Facts are stubborn things

> - o Instead, the team ignored reality, retreated back into their systems mentality to fix the problem, and:
>   - ▪ Changed the timing of the play.

- Added risk to the career of the quarterback.
- Required the offensive line to work overtime in the weight room.
- Compiled additional work instructions that have become so long and cumbersome, none of the players even bother to read them anymore.
  o For all of their efforts, they failed to address the real problem.
    - Personnel issues are always difficult and can never be fixed with a new system.

What if the Head Coach was totally locked into the systems mentality? He would call over his young Receiver's Coach for a brief conversation regarding team policy.

Head Coach: *"Do you see any way that we can redesign the play to accommodate for his lack of speed?"*

Rec. Coach: *"No matter how we draw up the play, he's simply too slow to execute at this level. We're asking other positions to make up for his weaknesses, and quite frankly it's causing a lot of friction in the locker room."*

➤ The all too predictable model for the company that puts their systems above their business is that they have a problem, and then upgrade their systems. They have another problem, and then upgrade their systems. They have another problem, and then upgrade their systems. They become unresponsive to market demands, profits suffer due to bloated overhead costs, they react by implementing a company-wide restructuring plan, and then jump back on the same treadmill. Back to our dysfunctional team:

Head Coach: *"Sounds like we need to add some sensitivity training to our calendar."* *He makes a note in his handheld computer.* *"Has he been through our 'run as fast as you can' program? Have we done everything we can to make sure that he's as fast as he can be?"*

Rec. Coach: *"I've been working with him all season, and he gets more coaching attention than anyone on the team. So much so, that we are neglecting a lot of our other players. The problem is, 'as fast as he can' isn't nearly fast enough."*

Head Coach: *"How long has he been with the team?"*

Rec. Coach: *"That's part of the problem, Coach, he has been with us nearly thirty years and, quite naturally, has slowed down a lot."*

Head Coach: *"Thirty years is a long time, young man. I'm not going to replace one of our valued players."*

➤ The problem that they have created is that if the receiver wanted to remain with the team for thirty years, they failed to develop his abilities off of the field where he has become a liability. They wasted the opportunity to grow him as a coach or scout when his physical abilities began to deteriorate twenty years earlier. Fortunately for your "progressive" coaching staff, the Defensive Coordinator has been eavesdropping and has a solution.

D.C.: *"I have an idea." He moves over next to them. "Our left tackle limped off the field after that last series, and it looks like he might be out for the rest of the game. Let's just move your receiver over there for right now."*

Head Coach: *"That's a great idea."*

Rec. Coach: *"But he only weighs 185 pounds. That's not fair to the rest of the offense, and our quarterback and running backs are likely to wind up in the hospital."*

Head Coach: *"Last time I checked, I'm still the Head Coach. If I say that he's playing offensive tackle, then he's playing offensive tackle. If there's a problem, we can just run* *everything away from him."*

D.C.: *"You have to have some faith in people," he self-righteously replies as he works to defend his suggestion. "Because of all of our recent problems completing passes, we have developed an excellent set of work instructions for the offensive line, and he may not be fast enough for you, but there is no debating that he's a fast reader."*

Head Coach: *"You just worry about your receivers. I trust that you have someone in mind to replace him?"*

Rec. Coach: *"I have someone ready to go who can run a 4.4-second forty; he will be perfect for the play that we have been struggling with," he says as the Offensive Coordinator joins the group.*

O.C.: *"Not for this game he won't. I just finished updating the playbook, which changed the timing for that play. I'll text message the other coaches for a meeting on Tuesday to determine if it makes sense to develop new work instructions so that your new receiver can run at fun speed in future games." He pulls out his handheld computer. "Until then, he's just going to have to run slower."*

Head Coach: *"What we really need to do is concentrate our play design to allow for success regardless of the speed of the receiver. Ideally, in a perfectly designed play, anyone could play receiver, quarterback, or along the offensive line." The Offensive and Defensive Coordinators nod their approval at his obviously enlightened coaching philosophy.*

➤ At this point, it's essential to take a breath and ask two questions:
  o How utterly ridiculous is this situation?
  o Even more ridiculous, how many times have you been

involved in an issue that followed the same train of thought, and no one objected?

➢ Because the team took so long getting around to dealing with the facts, they stopped developing the receiver along a path that fit his abilities, creating a significant personnel issue:
  o The player has been put in a position where failure is inevitable.
  o If he wanted to remain with the organization in another role, they have wasted nearly two decades, damaging his opportunity to succeed by accommodating him on the field.
  o The coaches have unfairly demanded that others on the team make up for his shortcomings, resulting in a disgruntled locker room.
    ▪ The fact that the team was ignoring his lack of speed didn't change the reality that he had a lack of speed.

➢ You aren't doing your employees any favors by leaving them in a situation where their skill set doesn't meet the demands of the job.
  o They know when they are failing.
  o Their co-workers know when they are failing.
  o Typically, it's only management that is in denial, and left unaddressed, you have just legitimized failure.
    ▪ It's time to grow up and run a professional organization.
    ▪ It's time to make auditing the people a priority.
➢ At the risk of alienating many readers, it's worth noting that it is

commonplace within organizations to promote individuals into system compliance positions who rarely have a resume packed with a long and distinguished list of accomplishments.

- o Once again, revealing management's actual commitment.
- o Oftentimes, the task falls to the employee whose most notable skill is moving from office to office throughout the day, pontificating on proper management practices, as opposed to actually accomplishing anything.
    - That said, when you identify the "perfect" person, ask these two questions:
    1.) Do his or her accomplishments clearly demonstrate an ability to improve the organization?
    2.) Would I be happier if this person left the company for another job?
    - "Yes" to question two is a strong clue that you need to start the selection process over or, better yet, reconsider the position.
- o Management frequently appoints people to compliance positions for no more noble reason than an attempt to shut them up.

Flaw – Lack of integrity

- ➤ When I owned my first company, I was always amazed that our ISO suppliers were invariably at the very top of the list when it came to quality, delivery, pricing, and service issues.
    - o The good part was that they always had textbook answers readily prepared for their failures.
    - o The bad news was that their answers rarely solved anything. However, they were able to check off a box in their paperwork, and proud of it.
        - In the meantime, their products and services remained junk, because their primary commitment wasn't to the business — it was to maintaining the systems

within their business. As long as they could check off their boxes, they were happy.
- o Beware of answers that sound like:
  - ▪ "We're an ISO company, so that sort of thing shouldn't happen."
  - ▪ "We'll put in a system to fix it."
  - ▪ "We've identified the root cause."
- o I feel so much better. Apparently, instead of complaining about the poor quality of their company, I should have presented them with a trophy.
  - ▪ Put it on your calendar; they will screw it up again, in the same manner, with the same excuses, and the same meaningless fix.
- o Warning — beware of the company that insists on showing you all of their plaques and awards; what you want to see are their world-class products and services.

Flaw – Management by fuzzy feeling

- ➢ Reality check — excess systems are not capable of being anything but an excess cost.
  - o The sales pitch of the person offering the enlightenment is always something along the lines of: "You can't afford not to."
    - ▪ Really, that's great news! Prove it.
  - o That is precisely the criteria that you would use for _**any other investment.**_
    - ▪ Why should management systems be exempt?
  - o If they can demonstrate the financial benefit, great, get started.
  - o Treat your systems like any other investment.
    - ▪ The "holier than thou" position will pay no bills and has no place in your business.

KEY - Business 101

- ➤ You may find that your customers will force your organization into adopting a specific formal system. If so, the key is:
  - o Never let your systems run your business. How can you tell if it's out of control?
    - ▪ The system becomes the actual business. The actual business becomes secondary to the systems.
    - ▪ TEST — If you ever hear that "the system won't let us do that," and it refers to something that would make you money, it's time to change the system.
    - ▪ TEST — Your internal paperwork:
      - • Helps the business perform better.
      - • Conforms to system demands despite the business.
    - ▪ TEST — Your people:
      - • Are they product/service experts?
      - • Are they systems experts?
  - o Your customer may demand you attain certain levels of certification; however, when it comes time to pay the bills, they will be nowhere in sight. They aren't going to pay them, and they aren't going to cosign for your debt.
    - ▪ They pay for your products and services, not your systems.

The coaches can't fix every problem by adding additional detail to the playbook. Statistics and charts make for good presentations, but the game is played on the field. Defensive players have to make tackles. Receivers need to get open and catch passes. Quarterbacks need to be able to read defenses and throw accurately. The coaches need to put the players in the best position to succeed. The team needs to have the best playbook possible, but come game time, the players need to be able to go out on the field and play to win.

- • *The team must have excellent players.*

- *The team must have committed players.*
- *The team must have players willing to take responsibility.*
- *The team must have a coaching staff that is willing to make difficult decisions about the players.*
- *The team must concentrate only on those actions that improve the team.*

Chapter **13**

It's Your Team
Never Let Your Customers Run Your Business

I t is essential that every company listen carefully to their customers. You must recognize that the customer is your source of revenue, and ignoring the wants and needs of your income stream is nothing short of foolish. However, that doesn't mean that you should automatically do what they tell you to do. Where you earn your paycheck is taking customer input and then making decisions relative to how your organization should invest their resources to maximize the potential of your company. The customer can make all of the demands that they want; it is your responsibility to determine if those demands will produce positive results for your organization. It is your responsibility to determine how your company can best go about meeting the needs of your customer. All too often, weak managers fall into the trap of letting their customers make critical decisions for their company because they either don't know what to do, or have failed to maintain a competitive position where they can effectively run their own company.

> ➤ This chapter is the logical follow-up to the warning of not allowing systems to blindly run your company. In the same manner, your

customer's goals and your goals are never the same, and you **_must never_** allow someone else to manage your business.

➤ Every organization is unique, and will have its own objectives.
  o The old saying, "The customer is always right" — really?
    ▪ What do they know about your business?
    ▪ What do they know about your employees? Suppliers? Financial situation?
      • The correct answer — little to nothing.
  o So, why would you allow them to run your business?

KEY – Be a professional

Consider our football team's customers. Who gives them money?

• *The fans:*
  o *First and foremost, they want their team to win.*
    ▪ *If they win, more fans come to the game, more merchandise is sold, more concessions are sold, and a better television contract can be negotiated.*
      • *The players, owners and the networks all stand to financially benefit.*
    ▪ *The fans would prefer that it be exciting, but a thrilling loss is not an acceptable alternative.*
    ▪ *The fans would like the game to be full of spectacular plays and big hits.*
      • *However, they come and cheer, and will spend their money, if their team wins.*
• *The networks:*
  o *They want high-scoring, close games.*
  o *They want games full of big plays and big hits.*
  o *They want a lot of offense.*
  o *They want every game to come down to the last play so that their audience watches until the very end.*
  o *The only time that they want to see the punter on the field*

is when the kick is returned for a touchdown.
- o *They love a QB controversy, and will even go out of their way to try and incite one.*
- o *The loud mouth receiver that wreaks havoc in the locker room is the first player to get an interview after the game.*
- o *The coach on the bubble helps to create high ratings.*
- ➢ It's impossible for two separate organizations to have goals that are always compatible with each other, and it is naive to manage with such an assumption.
  - o Your company should cooperate with other organizations when it's in your company's best interest.
  - o Other companies should cooperate with your organization when it's in their company's best interest.

If the team wins, it's obviously good for your team. However, the team's victory isn't in the best interest of everyone involved in the profession.

- • *The other team lost; so much for win-win, which will be reconsidered in the next chapter.*
- • *The win is good for the team's fans.*
- • *It may, or may not, be in the best interests of the network.*

  - o *If they won the game on a last-second field goal that kept everyone tuned in, it represents a win for the network.*
  - o *If they jumped out to a four-touchdown lead in the second quarter, and a large percentage of their audience turned the channel or went out to mow the yard, it represents a loss for the network.*
    - ▪ *Reality check — they simply don't care who wins.*
      - • *They are interested in maximizing the number of viewers for the entire game so that they can increase advertising revenue.*

KEY – Facts are stubborn things

The same analysis can be made for every big hit throughout the game:

- *Good for the team when they make the hits.*
- *Bad for the team when the opposition makes the hits.*
    - o *It's critical that their team avoids injuries if they are going to consistently win.*
- *Good for their fans when they make the hits.*
    - o *They even love when the home team takes big hits, as long as their favorite players aren't injured.*
- *Good for the network regardless of who is taking the hit.*
    - o *Not only does the audience love it, the big hits provide footage that can be utilized in pre- and post-game shows for the next week.*
        - ▪ *They would prefer that no "key" players be injured.*
            - • *Note the difference between key players to the team, and to the network:*
                - o *Team = a player who makes a significant contribution toward winning.*
                - o *Network = a highly visible player who draws fans and increases ratings.*

In a generic sense, they all want the market for professional football to expand. Beyond that common link, what is good for each group is very different. Many times, they are actually diametrically opposed. They each need to concentrate on managing their own organization.

- ➤ Your customers will try to tell you, "You must do this, and you must do that."
    - o Consider what they say; however, keep in mind that their

demands are aligned with their agenda, not yours, and will frequently prove counterproductive to your organization.

Fans will always call for the backup quarterback. They want to see the ball thrown more, but when it falls to the turf, they start grumbling about the play selection, question why the team abandoned the running game, and start calling for the coach to be fired.

Are these things really in the best interest of the team? The fans have the right to demand an entertaining team; however, the coach must do what is in the best interest of the team, because history has proven that the fans will fill the seats when the team wins. The network needs to cover the games that result in the highest ratings, but the coach would be foolish to try and manage the game to try and create a last-second field goal attempt to try and satisfy their objectives.

➤ Never allow someone else to spend your resources:
   o It's *your* money.
   o It's *your* time.
   o It's *your* future.
      ▪ They will not be there to bail out your bad investments and decisions.
         • Nor should they be.

KEY - Business 101

The fans may want the team to go for it on fourth and one, but if they fail, and it costs the team the game, they will boo the decision and criticize the execution of the players. By morning, they will fill the talk radio shows with scathing comments regarding the Head Coach's poor decision-making.

➤ If you are going to screw up your business, do it yourself. Don't let someone else do it for you.
   o What you ***must do*** is listen to your customers and seriously

consider what they say.

- o What you ***must do*** is run your business in the best interest of your company, because you understand it much better than your customers do, no matter what they may think.
    - You can count on this: the worse managed your customer is, the more likely it is that they are going to tell you what to do.

Flaw – Bad management

What trend will you invariably see with these fans? The less they know about the game, the more they challenge the decisions being made by the experts. I have found that the same can be said in the business world. Remember that the measurement of success ultimately comes down to wins.

- ➤ A common trait of companies that are incapable of running their own organization is that for some unexplainable reason, they are convinced that they can manage yours.
    - o I realize that it might seen to be unkind to pick on them, but a classic example of this is the North American Automotive Industry. They have been consumed with telling their suppliers how to run their businesses for years while their own companies have been imploding. They always wanted to tell their supply base:
        - This is your price.
        - This is your acceptable margin.
        - This is where you need to build a plant.
        - This is how you manage.
            - Someone needed to ask:

KEY – Does this make sense?

- o The companies that were rapidly losing market share, falling short of the global quality bar, and losing money at staggering levels had taken it upon themselves to tell everyone else how to properly manage a company.
  - There should be a better reason for an industry insisting that the laws of supply and demand be abandoned than "because we say so."

Flaw – Lack of integrity

- o What really would have helped their suppliers would have been if they put some of that effort into the mess they created within their own companies.
  - Thousands of employees might still be working, and hardworking suppliers who did nothing more than try to keep their domineering customers happy would still be solvent.
    - Pull for them to reestablish themselves because of the role they play in many communities across the country and the economy at large, but never forget the catastrophic negative effects that arrogant management can have.

Before this week's game, the coaching staff held meetings with a vocal group of upset fans and the networks. The fans demanded that the backup quarterback not only start the next game, but throw the ball deep at least once on every series. Clearly, this is more entertaining for them. The network negotiated a deal with the player's union to ensure that each team has at least one high-level malcontent on the roster so that they would have a constant stream of controversial news bites to dissect.

The team was informed that their player would be attending practice that very day; however, expect him to be a little late because he was currently holding a press conference to discuss the weaknesses of his new team. Ownership reinforced to the coaching staff that they would still be held accountable for winning, regardless of the problems created by any changes.

➢ What the customer has a right to **_demand_**, and **_demand_** is the correct term, is the best product or service at a fair price.
- o They have the right to demand constant improvement and input concerning how to improve their offerings.
- o You owe them an honest, professional business relationship.
- o They owe you an honest, professional business relationship.
    - ▪ That's it. Don't overcomplicate it.
➢ Your customers will make a lot of ideal statements that sound very nice. However, the reality is, what they want is:
- o A world-class product or service that provides **_their_** company with a competitive advantage.
- o They want the lowest cost so that they can increase **_their_** profits.
- o They want you to make unlimited investment for the benefit of **_their_** company.
- o They want you to invest large amounts of capital into research and development to benefit **_their_** company.
- o They may even claim that they want you to make a fair profit.
    - ▪ What they really want is for you to make **_their_** company more profitable.
        - • Which is fair.
        - • All parties need to be honest about it.
- o They don't care how much money you make; they simply would prefer that you don't go out of business because it would be inconvenient for **_their_** company.

There is a constant stream of unrelenting advice and criticism surrounding the Head Coach every waking moment of his day. Regardless of their lack of expertise, everyone thinks that they know what is best for the team. The challenge for the coach is to identify those few around him who are capable of making meaningful contributions to the objectives of the team. In the final judgment of his abilities, it becomes painfully simple:

- *If the team wins, the coach is a genius.*
- *If the team loses, the coach is an idiot.*

While both conclusions are obviously oversimplifications, it remains how the coach will be judged, and he must make certain that he is concentrating on what is best for his team. If the fans and networks are happy, that's great. However, that's not the coach's job. His responsibility is to win games.

Chapter **14**

Play to Win
Rethinking Win-Win

T he vast majority of us would prefer that the people around us throughout the day were happy, friendly, positive individuals. There is no denying that a cooperative working environment makes life a lot more pleasant. Furthermore, we would also prefer that the people we work with on a day-to-day basis liked us. There is a lot less friction in any profession when the employees not only get along, but also actually enjoy working together. The challenge to our happy workplace is when reality insists on making an uninvited appearance. It has a nasty habit of reminding us that we live in a highly competitive world with conflicting personalities, interests, agendas, and expectations. While it is noble to want to make everyone around us feel good, at those moments when I slip into that mind-set, I am reminded that even Jesus made no effort to accommodate everyone, and that being the case, it is probably far too ambitious of a goal for the rest of us. A much more realistic objective is to pursue what's best, regardless of how those around you might feel about it.

> ➢ Win-win: what a nice, warm, fluffy concept.
>> o It's a wonderful ideal, and as such, worthy of consideration.

- Primarily, it makes me think of puppies and rainbows.

Flaw – Management by fuzzy feeling

➢ To objectively consider this philosophy, which in many organizations is considered an unimpeachable way of life, it's essential that you separate internal win-win from external win-win.
  o Internally, you must relentlessly work toward win-win.
    - The key is that it's a journey full of two steps forward, one step back.
  o The most obvious example is that compensation must provide incentive for the employee to contribute to the company in a manner greater than their package.
    - Pay packages must benefit the business.
      • Anything less would be a bad investment.

KEY – Be a professional

- Pay packages must be fair to the employee.
  • Anything less is unsustainable and will result in an unmotivated employee, or an employee who will eventually look elsewhere. Potentially with a competitor.
➢ Even accepting win-win as an internal objective, you must recognize that employee satisfaction is not a static activity. Your employees aren't long-term contracts, products, services, or even boxes on a grand organizational chart. They are people with unique ambitions, insecurities, challenges, and opportunities both inside and outside of the organization. As a result, they can never be treated as a homogeneous group with identical needs.
  o The only way to successfully realize this objective within

your company is to pursue it relentlessly, and that mandates that you consistently engage those around you.

For the team, this is where internal win-win comes into play in its purest form. The team must pay the player the salary that the marketplace has established. If they fail to do so, he will move to another team and become a competitor, potentially forcing them to fill the vacancy by overpaying or compromising performance. The player must produce results that are representative of his compensation package. If he fails to deliver, the team will waste little time in demanding that the contract be renegotiated, or may choose to release the player.

➤ Throughout this process, you can't ignore that employee satisfaction includes much more than what they take home in their paychecks:
  - o Opportunities for advancement; top performers always demand this.
  - o Working conditions.
  - o Vacations.
  - o A sense of contribution.
  - o Benefits.
  - o Flexibility.
  - o Challenging assignments.

The quarterback listened carefully as his agent read through the key points of the contract offer. Changing teams after seven seasons in the league represented the single biggest career decision that he had been faced with to date. The salary was competitive; the guaranteed money met his expectations. However, the one sentence that he was looking for was conspicuously missing. He could stay with his current team and mentor their first-round draft choice if he wanted to carry a clipboard during games; what he wanted was the opportunity to compete for the starting position.

➤ While you drive toward your noble internal objectives, you can't ignore the realities of win-win. Perfect situations rarely

materialize, resulting in a state of constant compromises.
- o As was pointed out above, if satisfactory compensation can't be negotiated, you must deal with the issue.
  - Is the employee going to underperform or leave?
  - How are you going to keep them motivated?
  - What is your plan if they leave?
  - Are the employee's expectations unrealistic?
  - Are your expectations unrealistic?
- o Budget cuts may produce a win for the bottom line, but the departments that sacrifice funding, or employees who lose jobs, will have a hard time seeing their win.
- o Launching new product lines are essential to maintain the viability of the company, but when they result in cancelled vacations and increased travel schedules, the win can be difficult to swallow for many employees.
- o Life is never so easy that reality fits into nice, neat win-win or no-deal boxes that others would have you believe in.
  - You need to continually work toward this objective internally; however, it's much more likely that you will be presented with:
    - Boxes for: these are the corporate goals, this is the timeline, we must do this.
  - Your job is to create as many wins as possible and keep the organization moving forward.
- ➤ Externally, there needs to be a change of mind-set concerning the win-win principle.
  - o Over the years, the practice has evolved into one of the most abused and disingenuous philosophies ever peddled.
  - o Rather than a tool of cooperation, manipulative negotiators frequently use it as a weapon of intimidation.

Flaw – Lack of integrity

- o When you find people relentlessly insisting on the concept regardless of the situation, you will oftentimes will find one of three things:

- Individuals not directly responsible for profit.
- One company (large customer) trying to shove their enlightenment down the throat of a second company (small supplier).
    - Note that the flow of new programs always moves in the same direction.
- Within an organization, a non-profit-generating department attempting to instruct another department regarding competent management techniques.

Take a moment and briefly return to the points concerning the teams and television networks examined in the previous chapter. The networks love:

- *Any, and every, quarterback controversy that they can incite.*
- *They go out of their way to encourage the loudmouth receiver who wreaks havoc in the locker room.*
- *They endlessly discuss the coach who is perceived to be on the bubble, even if the controversy is purely of their own invention.*

All of these circumstances are a win for the network. However, they clearly represent a lose scenario for the team. Revisiting our prior example, the network must cover the games in their best interest. The team must manage each game in its best interest. Cooperate with each other wherever possible to expand the overall audience for the game, but always keep in mind that this cooperation doesn't provide you the option of ignoring the reality that each organization has its own set of selfish objectives. Ultimately, each group must be responsible for its individual success, regardless of the success of the other parties.

KEY – Facts are stubborn things

➤ The economics of win–win expose some basic flaws;
  o You are down to negotiating price for your product.
    ▪ Your cost is $1,000.
    ▪ The customer is currently paying $1,500 from your leading competitor.
    ▪ At a selling price of $1,400, you profit $400, and the customer saves $100. Both parties win. What could possibly be better?

KEY – Never get too comfortable

  o Consider some very complex financial analysis before proceeding:
    ▪ For your company, is $450 profit better than $400 profit?
      • It still represents a savings for your customer.
    ▪ For your customer, would a $200 savings be better than the $100 on the table?
      • It still represents a profit for your company.
  o These options all would appear to be win-win; however, clearly there are degrees of win-win where one company does better than the other.
    ▪ If both parties win, do the details really matter? After all, we are all feeling pretty good about the negotiations and ourselves.

Flaw – Management by fuzzy feeling

- *The players are not experts at managing the team, the networks, or the companies paying for the advertisements. They need to focus on playing the game to the best of their abilities, and let their agents concentrate on their contract negotiations.*
- *The owners are not capable of playing the game, and aren't familiar with the intricacies of the network's or advertisers' businesses. They need to focus on negotiating the best contracts that they can with the players and networks.*
- *The networks are not capable of playing the game, and are not in a position to manage the teams or the advertisers. They need to focus on negotiating the best possible contracts with the league, and the highest possible rate from the advertisers.*

Why would any of these respective groups believe that there is a single outcome that maximizes everyone's success? Only by accepting simpleminded management.

Flaw – Bad management

➢ The details are always what matters in every business.
   o Share prices swing on the profitability of organizations.
   o Capital to invest for long-term viability is at stake.
   o The careers of the people involved in the transaction will be determined.
   o Bonuses are awarded, or not.
   o Promotions will be handed out to the most successful employees.
      ▪ Maximizing your win will improve the level of your company's success, as well as determine your future.
   o Win-win cannot be blindly adopted regardless of the circumstances.

- It's just too simple of an all-encompassing philosophy to be anything short of intellectually lazy.
o As you are trying to make everyone happy, keep asking:

KEY – Does this make sense?

- Does the concept of trying to make everyone happy **_ever_** make sense in any aspect of your life?
o Work toward an agreement where both sides win, i.e., are satisfied with the deal.
o Look for opportunities where everyone benefits.
  - However, remember, regardless of how the other organization feels, your company must win.
    - It's hard enough making the right decisions for your company. Don't be so self-righteous that you believe that you know what is best for everyone.
o You have enough to worry about.
o If you don't have faith that the company you are dealing with can manage their own affairs, you need to reconsider doing business with them.
  - Deal with companies where you believe that their management is competent enough to manage themselves.
  - Go light on the new-age fluff management being peddled by a lot of people who have never actually managed a business.
o When you feel the urge coming on, take a quick trip to the local animal shelter and rescue a puppy instead.

Flaw – Management by fuzzy feeling

For the good of everyone involved in professional football, players need to commit to playing to win, the franchise needs to concentrate on maintaining profitability, and the networks need to strive for the highest ratings possible. For all of their good intentions, every player can't be successful every game when it's the objective of the offense to score and the defense to stop them from scoring. Every team can't win every game. Every broadcast isn't going to maximize ratings when one team jumps out to a large lead and takes advantage of the opportunity to rest their marquee players. Some players, and some teams, are going to have more success than others. No coach ever wants to see a competitor's franchise fold or relocate due to a lack of fan support, but that doesn't mean that he will go easy during a game. His team must play to win.

Chapter 15

What's the Score?
Know Your Numbers

W hether or not a business is successful is ultimately determined based on the numbers that it produces. The numbers represent the scoreboard for your company. How well you executed, how perfect the game plan was, or even if you were unfairly defeated won't be considered when time runs out. All that will be remembered is the final score. That reality can never be used as an excuse for not operating in a responsible manner, but likewise, being socially responsible is not an excuse for generating substandard results. Like it or not, numbers are the language of business, and you, and everyone around you, must be able to speak that language clearly and concisely if you want to be consistently successful.

➢ The management deficiency of not knowing your numbers frequently goes hand in hand with the manager following the hope strategy.
   o They hope that the numbers turn out good enough to get them through another month.
   o Alternatively, these managers are prone to be lazy, which invariably leads them directly down the path toward ignoring the numbers.

- It's the natural outgrowth of the flaw:

Flaw – Ask how hard something is

o These managers don't want to put the energy into effective leadership and, as a result, are capable only of damaging the organization and everyone around them.
- Every individual is either adding to, or subtracting from, the value of the business. There are no other alternatives.

Flaw – Lack of integrity

➢ The numbers your business is producing are always telling you something, but you must pay attention to them. They won't seek you out to highlight an issue or present an opportunity.
  o They patiently wait for you to analyze their meaning, consider the story that they are telling, and then initiate appropriate action.
➢ Numbers are a direct result of actions, or the lack thereof.
  o More precisely, good numbers are the result of good decisions.
    - This is particularly true over the long term. Even if a company gets lucky and generates good numbers for a short period of time, they will not maintain quality results without consistently making good decisions.
  o Bad numbers are the result of bad decisions or, even more frequently, inaction as you stand still while the world rapidly evolves all around you.
  o It can also be true that bad numbers are the result of a poor economy or deteriorating market conditions. However, you

can't get away with latching onto that excuse just because it's convenient.

Flaw – Debating if change is good or bad

- You are paid to make difficult decisions and develop strategies even in the most difficult of times. It's easy to manage a company when everything is going well.
  o Any organization that has survived for a lengthy period has faced, and conquered, challenges that resulted in some of their competitors going out of business.
    - If your company hasn't faced obstacles of this magnitude yet, they will.

The Head Coach developed a game plan that took the predictable Arizona weather into consideration. It was the perfect environment for the wide-open offense that they had implemented in the off-season. Inexplicitly, a torrential downpour has arrived at the stadium just before kickoff and, looking at the forecasts, appears to have settled in for the afternoon. It may not be the coach's fault that a bizarre twist of nature has rolled in; however, it remains the coach's responsibility to deal with the circumstances and adjust the game plan accordingly. He will be held accountable for the score regardless of the weather.

➤ Uncover the messages behind the numbers. Keep asking:

KEY – Does this make sense?

o Never stop digging into the numbers.
o Never stop challenging the numbers.
  - This commitment, in equal measures, is both

essential and endless.
- ➤ Typically, the problem of not understanding the numbers manifests itself in managers who fail in multiple aspects of leadership.

Flaw – Bad management

- o A less friendly assessment, management is incompetent.
  - ▪ They are afraid of the scorecard because they don't know how, or don't posses the energy, to improve the numbers.
- ➤ Take a positive perspective; the numbers help to expose your weaknesses, as well identifying your strengths.
  - o Every organization has both, regardless of whether they acknowledge them or not.
    - ▪ Expose your weaknesses, address them, and move on to what's next.
    - ▪ Exploit your strengths to their full potential.
- ➤ My promise to managers everywhere — ignore the numbers, and over time, they will deteriorate.
  - o Consistently good numbers are a lot of work, not an accident.
    - ▪ Maintaining quality numbers is extremely difficult; however, it remains the objective. It's precisely what management is paid to do.
- ➤ We have all heard the managers who claim "not to be a numbers person."
  - o Or the ever popular "do good things, and the numbers will take care of themselves."

Flaw – Management by fuzzy feeling

- o It sounds nice, and even makes sense as long as you don't think too deeply. As a result of this, the individual usually gets away with their proclamations for a while.

- After all, doing something positive is preferable to doing nothing.
  - At least you are increasing the odds of something good developing.

O.C.:   *"I think that we should just keep running these ten plays in the same order all game because that's what the players are accustomed to doing," he says to the Head Coach.*

Occasionally, a play will result in some level of success because it accidentally aligned with the defensive formation and the game situation. That doesn't make it a professional plan of action.

- o Nevertheless, for some indefensible reason, this is a cop-out that a lot of managers get away with.
  - Far too often, for their entire career.
- o In numerous organizations, mediocrity is willing to accept mediocrity.
  - Being a real leader requires that you not only accomplish things, you continually identify the most critical objectives to accomplish and attack them.

Take the same ten plays from the previous example and begin matching them up against the weaknesses of the defense and the situation on the field. Instantly, that one change has mathematically increased the chances for success by replacing hope with analyzing strengths and exploiting weaknesses. It still isn't ideal because the playbook is too limiting, but at least the team is now moving in a positive direction.

- ➤ Critical analysis that results in improving your organization is impossible without a thorough understanding of the numbers and what drives them.

- o It forces managers to get out of their comfort zone and deal with the challenges of the business.

KEY – Be a professional

- o Without this discipline, your business will slip into the pattern of running from one improvement project to another without ever determining which actions will result in the greatest improvement.
  - Once again, leadership is abdicating the management of the company over to hoping for the best.

The team was locked into improvements without asking:

- *Is the play-calling the most appropriate for the situation?*
- *Is the execution good enough to succeed?*
- *The issue: is this the best course of action to increase the team's opportunity to win the game?*

The team keeps improving their fundamentals, which sounds wonderful, but it's not translating into wins. While constant incremental improvement is critical to the success of any organization, the days where that was enough are gone. The team cannot identify continuous improvement as the goal. It must establish improvement to the level where they win as the goal.

By the end of the season, the offensive line was twice as effective as compared to the season opener. Quarterback sacks were lowered from an average of eight per game the first half of the season, to four per game the second half. That's great; they started the season as a complete disaster in pass protection, and ended as a lesser disaster, but still a disaster. The bottom line, the team surrenders too many sacks to complete, and furthermore, there isn't a quality quarterback in the league willing to step under center and jeopardize their career unless the situation is corrected.

- *The improvement appears impressive on a colorful chart displayed in the meeting room; however, graphs don't take the field and block three-hundred-pound defensive linemen.*

➤ Reality — Improvements that are insufficient to win are just one more excuse for not committing to understanding the numbers.

Ignoring the numbers is the equivalency of our football team calling a play without knowing the down or distance. They keep running the same play over and over, diligently working at improving, but failing to consider if their strategy is capable of winning. The first time, the result is a five-yard loss. Gradually, throughout the game, they keep getting better. By the end of the game, they run the play for the twentieth time and finally manage to gain a half yard.

What an incredible improvement! Time to hand out the promotions and bonus checks! The problem was, the coaching staff never examined the numbers in light of wins or losses. After spending most of the game continually losing yardage on every play, they finally managed a positive gain. Who cares? Certainly not their opponent; the game was decided in the first quarter. It's impossible to win a game gaining a half yard on twentieth carry. Not only shouldn't the coaches be happy with their remarkable improvement, whoever is calling the plays needs to be shown the door, and fast.

➤ Somehow, in our overeducated, plan of the month, self-declared sophisticated business world, many companies subscribe to this logic on a regular basis.
  - o Charting the trend line would not only demonstrate tremendous improvement, it would justify additional investment into this cutting-edge strategy.
  - o Carrying the "proven" continuous improvement trend line forward, the strategy would eventually result in increasingly positive results every time the philosophy was

implemented, and after years of hard work and millions of dollars in capital investment, the company could score on every play.

- Not only is this unreasonable, it's impossible.
  o Regardless, I have seen assumptions with equally ludicrous projections made by experienced managers.

Flaw – Bad management

  o Worse yet, they frequently are not only left unchallenged, but applauded.
➢ As if this wasn't enough, many organizations would examine the trends and rush to mimic the success throughout all areas of the company.
  o Focus groups would be initiated to expand the results across all departments, regardless of the relevancy.
  o Members of this remarkable department would be used to train employees from other areas in their obviously insightful strategies.
  o The overachieving manager of the "run the same play on every down" department would be promoted to a board position with the commensurate compensation package and corporate perks afforded to those capable of such progressive thinking.
    - All because the leadership is ignoring the significance of managing the business to win.
➢ After all of the work is done, the customer is satisfied, and the budget approved, your business is only as good as its numbers.
  o A cold reality, nonetheless, reality.

KEY – Facts are stubborn things

If the team continues to lose but statistically improves in every aspect of the game, the Head Coach and his staff may be able to buy another season from the ownership and General Manager to turn the statistics into wins, but everyone involved understands the rules. Ultimately, professional teams are always measured in terms of wins and losses, and there is no escape. It's a performance-based business.

➢ In the same manner, professional businesses are measured in terms of profits and losses.
  o Happy employees are great.
    ▪ It's impossible to be successful long term without them.
  o Satisfied customers should always be the objective.
    ▪ Unhappy customers will become ex-customers.
  o World-class products and services, essential.
    ▪ You must have them if you plan on remaining viable.
  o Dominant market positions are an unceasing objective.
    ▪ They allow you to achieve pricing power.
  o Social and environmental responsibility must be uncompromising.
    ▪ You must make profit with integrity.

KEY - Business 101

➢ All of this considered, without profit, the other objectives don't matter.

• *Without wins, it's time for new coaches and players.*

➢ The second leg of this deficiency is not understanding the numbers.
  o Management is receiving adequate details, but has no idea what actions to take based on the story that the numbers are telling.

- This never ceases to frustrate me — key managers are allowed to get away with not understanding the language of their profession.
  o I find them in unrepentantly large numbers scattered throughout the corporate world. Frequently, even within financial disciplines.
    - Many with what should be top quality educations and resumes.
  o We may all have our specialties, but the objective of business is to make money, and the only way to measure progress is with numbers. So, how can anyone involved in business not develop at least a fundamental understanding of the numbers and what drives them within their particular business?
    - Every manager must be aware of how their job impacts the results — the bottom line results.
      • If you have no effect, why are you there?
  o There is no excuse.

KEY – Never get too comfortable

➤ At times, employees go into new positions without thoroughly understanding how the numbers affect their area of responsibility. However, that isn't a reason to remain uneducated.
  o Understanding this aspect of your new position is job one.
  o The numbers can be extremely complex, but the fundamentals that drive an organization are not. Yet, many managers rely on someone else to tell him or her what the numbers mean.
    - Generally, that's a very bad idea. You must have at least enough understanding to know which questions to ask, and when the answers aren't sound.
  o Learn everything you can about the numbers.

- o Make sure that you understand:
  - Where they come from.
  - How to get them.
  - Why they are important.
  - What's not important (stop doing it).
    - The devil is always in the details.

After several losing seasons, the team finally decided to make the commitment to start acknowledging the scoreboard throughout the game in an effort to make adjustments in a timelier manner. Unfortunately, the Head Coach doesn't understand the significance of the numbers on the scoreboard, and can't tell the difference between the score and the time remaining in the game. He now has access to all of the numbers that he needs, but still can't make the correct adjustments because the information is useless without context. He must have the ability to understand the relationship between what is taking place on the field, and what the numbers are telling him.

Moving to the next level, there would be little benefit if he understands only part of the scoreboard; proper adjustments still can't be consistently implemented. After being sent to a class on comprehending scoreboards, he can now confidently look up and see that they are down by a touchdown. However, if the only numbers he is familiar with are the score, he is missing essential pieces of information that will impact every play call.

- *Are there three quarters left in the game, or three seconds?*
  - o *This will dramatically affect his next decision.*
- *It's fourth down and a foot; do they go for it or punt?*
  - o *If they make their decision based solely on the score, the only way to be right is to be lucky.*
    - *Are they on their own ten-yard line or about to move in and score?*
    - *Is it the first quarter or the last ten seconds of the game?*
    - *Are they ahead by twenty or trailing by twenty?*
  - o *In this case, the decision to go for it could strategically be:*

- *A gamble with little downside, but with the potential to pull out a victory.*
- *An easy decision dictated by the score and time.*
- *A strategic blunder with no upside, but a huge downside that could cost the team the game and, justifiably, the coach's job.*
  - *The numbers on the scoreboard are all interrelated, and only understanding the significance of some of them is nearly as dangerous as not understanding any of them.*

➢ Not understanding the numbers in your business is no less egregious.
  - You will never have perfect information to make a decision, but that doesn't mean you don't dig for all of the data that you can get.

➢ Not understanding the numbers is typically where you will find the "Big Picture Guy."

Flaw – Management by fuzzy feeling

- They can't be bothered with the details. It's fourth and a foot, and they have a feeling that this is the time to go for the end zone. "You have to roll the dice and go with your gut sometimes."
  - That is an unacceptable cop-out; learn what is going on around you.
    - Invest the time.

KEY – Be a professional

- Reality — this is a common attitude that should be a flashing red light. You are dealing with someone who is out of touch with what is going on around them and, worse

yet, refuses to take the initiative to learn.
- Big picture numbers are wonderful, but they are derived from adding up all of the smaller numbers.

In the press conference after the game, the Head Coach was feeling good about the twenty-seven points that they managed to score; however, during questioning, it became obvious that he had no idea if it was the offense, defense, or special teams that actually put the points on the board. How can he possibly plan for the next game? This coach would universally be considered incompetent. Why would anyone consider the many managers with a similar grasp of the details be considered any less incompetent?

➢ You **_must_** pay attention to, **_and_** understand, the numbers, if you want to be an effective manager. The intricacies of finances can be complex; however, the fundamentals are not, and everyone must be able to interpret what they are saying.
➢ If your staff refuses to learn these fundamentals:
  o Communicate their importance and why you will insist on an understanding.
  o Work with them to gain competence.
  o If they choose not to cooperate:
    - Provide them with the opportunity to pursue a career that better lines up with their limited interests.

Throughout the game, the coaching staff must be able to examine what's taking place, understand why it's happening, and make the necessary adjustments to give the team the best chance for success. After the game, the staff needs to be able to not only evaluate the entire game plan, but also break down the details of every play in an effort to correct mistakes and begin preparing for the next game. It's a never-ending cycle if they are committed to providing their team with the best opportunity to win on a consistent basis. There is no room for a coach who takes little interest in the final score, or the details that resulted in the score.

156

Chapter 16

Learn from Every Play
Face Reality

O ne of the most common traits of weak managers is that they make plans based on what they want reality to be, rather than what it actually is. Many times, this habit is a result of someone at a higher level mandating performance targets that represent little more than a wish list. The pronouncement comes down from above that all product lines need to show a minimum of twenty percent annual growth rate throughout the planning cycle. Oftentimes, this type of decree is commonplace within a company that has created an environment where only the managers signing up to the mandate will receive individual promotions or adequate investment consideration. What the company undoubtedly will get is a plan full of twenty percent growth projections, and a detailed list of ill-conceived actions targeted at phantom goals.

If management honestly believes that twenty percent growth is essential, they need to examine each product line for viability and then develop targets and plans accordingly. Objective analysis may force them to accept that twenty percent growth is unrealistic from their current offerings, which would indicate that they need to develop new product lines, or consider acquisitions to achieve the growth targets. Conversely, they may discover that they were setting their targets too low and creating an environment where the organization was allowed to underachieve.

Our pretentious manager needs to realize that markets and execution determine growth rates, not directives from above. Consider a company that specialized in manufacturing carburetors for the automotive industry. They could demand all of the growth they wanted; however, the reality was that regardless of how good their plans were, how precisely they were executed, how much productivity improved, or even if they exceeded expectations in every conceivable quality measurable, their market was about to go the way of the dinosaur. Their only chance for survival was to face this reality and then utilize their considerable strengths and abilities to change the direction of the company. What they did not have time for was to waste a single hour trying to meet the unrealistic demands of someone in management insisting on an alternative reality.

> ➢ Dealing with circumstances as they actually are would seem obvious to any professional; however, when managers don't know what actions to take, it frequently is because they fail to make an effort to determine what the fundamental issues are plaguing the organization, such as:
>   - o The markets are deteriorating.
>   - o Costs are growing too quickly.
>   - o Offshore competition is eating away at margins.
>   - o Overhead is out of line.
> ➢ Once again, this is frequently the same manager who hopes things get better (notice how often this manager surfaces).
>   - o They fear reality, because once they have faced it, they will have to deal with it, and that might prove difficult or painful.

Flaw – Ask how hard something is

It does no good to ignore that their deep threat runs a 5.9-second forty-yard dash. Regardless of what they attempt to do around him to hide his weaknesses, his speed is a liability that will limit the effectiveness of the entire team. By default, they ask for more than the receiver is capable of, and more than is fair from the rest of the offense in an effort to overcome his lack of talent.

KEY – Facts are stubborn things

➢ If your company is similar to most, a trip to the Human Resource office will likely reveal that your problem employee's last performance evaluation was satisfactory or better.
   o The longer that you deny reality, the more painful the remedy becomes.
➢ This denial of reality is a result of managers who:
   o Aren't comfortable with change, so they don't change.
   o Don't like change, so they don't change.
   o Fear change, so they don't change.
   o Lack the competence to identify when changes need to be made, so they don't change.
      ▪ When the predictable difficult times arrive, these weak leaders will fall back into what they know best, becoming so immersed that they create a situation where they can't find the time to deal with any real issues.
         • They delude themselves into believing that they are working on the critical issues of the organization, when they are actually running away from them.

Flaw – Lack of integrity

➢ I once consulted a senior manager who was facing multiple issues in personnel, an exploding cost base, and an information system meltdown. His response was to become deeply involved in the new warehouse layout and procurement of a racking system because of his background in distribution.

- o It was less painful to ignore the real challenges and create urgent issues within a discipline where he was more comfortable.
    - If they come from sales, they will concentrate on sales.
    - If they come from engineering, they will concentrate on engineering.
    - If they come from finance, they will concentrate on finance.
        - You get the point.
- o It's much easier to slide back into areas of comfort, rather than dig into the details of uncovering and addressing the real issues, irrespective of the discipline or how difficult it might personally be.
    - Real leaders can't be afraid to uncover the key issues regardless of where they may appear.

KEY – Be a professional

The defense is terrible, but the Head Coach is an ex-offensive coordinator. The weak coach will flee from the defensive issues, even if he gives them lip service at the press conferences, and begin spending a disproportionate amount of time with the offense because that is his area of comfort. He isn't comfortable with fixing the problem, so he looks to fix any problem.

Head Coach: "We're giving up forty points a game, so clearly, our new objective has to be to score at least forty-one points," he insightfully proclaims at the staff meeting to kick off their weekly preparation.

A professional will deal with the facts and begin addressing the reality that his defense clearly is inferior. This will always involve the coach learning more about the defense if his experience has primarily been on the offensive side of the ball, potentially, even coming to the conclusion that additional expertise needs to be brought in. The quality coach will ensure that there is someone involved in leading the defense who is competent, and then will work through the problems with that coach. No Head Coach who is afraid to bring in strong assistants will ever be a success. The only reasons for him not to bring in help where needed are:

- *Insecurity*
- *Arrogance*
- *Incompetence*

Flaw – Bad management

> Many times, you will find that these weak managers have been pursuing the same actions, regardless of situation, not only in their current position, but also in every job they have ever held.
> - They're a hammer, so they treat everything like a nail.

Head Coach: "The four-wide receiver set was unstoppable two years ago, so let's just keep doing it."

Problem: this week's game is in a snowstorm, and their opponent is number one in the league against the pass, while proving incapable of stopping the run. The team wants to continue to exploit their strengths, but it would be foolish to ignore the weather and the strengths and weaknesses of their opponent for the upcoming game. With the snow coming down in sheets, the quarterback has repeatedly communicated that he can't see the receivers downfield. The receivers have confirmed that they can't see the quarterback, and even if there is a brief lull in the snow, the winds are gusting up to fifty miles per hour and won't allow for an accurate pass.

➢ Facing reality demands that we continually examine what we are doing, and how we are doing it.

    o Your company has been extremely successful with a product line that is very highly engineered, and the only other player in the market maintains a pricing policy of only selling products with a fat margin.

    o In an effort to expand your business, you have recently entered into a fast-growing market that appears positioned to expand twenty-five percent a year for the next eight to ten years.

        ▪ The difference in this market is that it is a relatively simple product to produce, there are already six competent competitors, and several more appear poised to enter the market within the next year. As a result, margins that are already thin will remain under pressure.

    o If your company adopts the philosophy that it wants to maintain the margins that it has become accustomed to within its engineered product line, it will fail in this developing market where a premium position doesn't exist.

        ▪ The rules in this market are different, and adopting the same strategy will not alter that fact.

    o Your company is either going to have to compete in this market based on price and accept more modest margins, or they are going to continually be frustrated with the results, and make poor decisions based on flawed assumptions.

The coaching staff cannot ignore the weather just because it is inconvenient and would result in committing to some extra hours to change their game plan.

Flaw – Debating if change is good or bad

➢ Deal with problems as they surface, where they surface.

    o Deal with them as quickly as possible, then move on to what is next.

Watching tape in the off-season, it became obvious that their offensive line was too small for a consistently effective running game. One option would be to change the offensive scheme to better match the skills of the current players. Alternatively, they could begin the process of replacing the current line with bigger players. In either case, the deficiency that the team's offensive objectives don't line up with their players' abilities must be addressed, and decisions need to be made to effect change.

A second challenge that must be addressed is that they are over the salary cap heading into the new season and, as a result, in no position to bring in some urgently needed free agents to plug holes along the defensive line. To be successful, they are going to be forced to examine the compensation of all of the current players on the roster. Are they worth what they are being paid? If not, they may need to renegotiate contracts where possible. This doesn't necessarily mean just taking the easy route and cutting pay across the board, which is extremely demotivating, but finding ways to restructure contracts in a manner that is fair to both the players and the organization. The incentives need to be realigned to ensure that the team is getting value at every position. In order to address this shortfall, they may be forced to consider the painful prospect of releasing underachieving players.

A final obstacle identified during the off-season was that the rest of their conference has become a lot faster over the past two seasons, and the result has been increased mismatches that their opponents are exploiting. In the near term, they may be faced with adjusting game plans to try and minimize the liabilities caused by their lack of speed. However, it's clear that they need to start drafting and signing faster players if the team is going to consistently compete. Once again, what they know for certain is that their team cannot sit still; speed is a deficiency that needs to be improved if they are going to be successful.

➢ The good thing about facing reality is that it forces your organization to adapt and improve.
    o You must continually adapt if you are going to survive.

> I once worked with a company that reported exceptional charges on an annual basis, which always seems a strange description for a yearly event that was more accurately described as predictable, rather than exceptional.
>
> o They chose to ignore the reality that they were regularly taking large write-offs, and then emphasized the quality of the remaining numbers when they reported their results to investors.

Flaw – Lack of integrity

o Someone needed to ask, "What are we doing wrong that causes us to keep taking large write-offs?"

KEY – Does this make sense?

- They never did.
- They kept taking exceptional costs year after year.
  - Their stock, as predictably as their "exceptional costs," underachieved and eventually tanked.

The Head Coach settles in behind the microphone at the post-game press conference after a tough loss:

Reporter: *"Coach, how can you continue to play a quarterback who struggles to complete fifty percent of his passes? He consistently has the lowest completion percentage of any starter in the league."*

Head Coach: *"I don't think that is necessarily an accurate reflection of his success. If you re-calculate his completion percentage after eliminating the throws that hit the referee, which as you all know in his case is nearly twenty percent of the time, it leaves him with the completion percentage without outside interference. This single adjustment in mind, he's actually one of the league leaders in completion percentage."*

➤ Results are results. If a manager is continually writing things off, it should not be classified as exceptional.
  o It should be classified as poor management.

Flaw – Bad management

  o Reality doesn't care about your plans, agendas, or timelines. It just keeps evolving, and it has an unforgiving habit of:
    ▪ Rewarding those who evolve with it.
    ▪ Punishing those who refuse to adapt.

The forecast calls for a snowstorm to bring winds out of the north at fifty miles per hour, with a wind chill of minus twenty at kickoff. The team specializes in having a potent passing attack. Standing on the sideline during the game as the wind and snow whip around the Head Coach and demanding that his team maintains its league-leading passing efficiency won't miraculously result in completed passes. It's a better assumption that if the quarterback has told the coach that he can't see his receivers, no matter how much he may like the game plan, circumstances have rendered it worthless.

Whether the coach likes the conditions or not is completely irrelevant. Furthermore, it's not worth discussing the problems that it's creating. It's time to pull all of the coaches together for an emergency session. The game plan that they worked on all week, and were so proud of, just went into the garbage. The coaching staff is paid to win games, and that requires acting professionally and dealing with the reality taking place on the field.

Chapter **17**

Eliminate Distractions
The Age of the Internet

In a historically short duration, the Internet made the leap from a novelty item to an integral part of the modern world. It seemed as though we woke up one morning, and suddenly, the planet had become a much smaller place than the night before. The Internet represents an amazingly powerful tool that has forever redefined all of the rules concerning communications, education, information, marketing, and research, just to name a few of the more high-profile disciplines. When we reflect back on this period of history, there will be a distinct line of separation dividing the period before, and after, the Internet became mainstream.

Some rules of life remain consistent regardless of how dramatically the world may shift. The more upside something has, the more downside it has. Invariably, investments with the greatest profit potential typically offer the threat for an equally spectacular failure. The Internet offers no exception from this time-proven reality. The ability to communicate, along with instant access to information, provides the opportunity to significantly increase the productivity of most organizations. Simultaneously, you have just placed that greatest single distraction mankind could create at your employees' fingertips. Like any aspect of your business, it is essential that you take responsibility for properly managing it.

- ➤ I would like to start right off and identify what the Internet honestly represents to most companies — a significant potential cost savings that management is responsible for capturing.
  - o Limit the Internet. More precisely, limit the Internet to productive uses that help the company reach its objectives.
    - ▪ It's a tool that has grown completely out of control at many companies.
  - o Rather than considering it on its own island, hold the Internet to the same level of accountability that you would any other tool.
    - ▪ It isn't just about the Internet; it's about managing all of the potential distractions at the workplace.
  - o What is particularly discomforting is that most companies that I work with realize that Internet abuse is a costly problem.
    - ▪ However, as we examined in the previous chapter, many managers simply choose to not face the problem because it might result in a confrontation.

Flaw – Bad management

- ➤ Return to the fundamentals and accept the Internet as a tool at the workplace, because that is precisely what it is.
  - o If your employees needed a hammer, you would make sure that they had a quality hammer. That doesn't infer that you would allow them to carry hammers around with them throughout the day, banging on desks and walls, just because it was beneficial for an hour in the morning.

KEY – Does this make sense?

➤ A sorry excuse that I have repeatedly heard managers fall back on is that unlimited access to the Internet is a reality of the modern world, and personal use is unavoidable.
  - o Go back and reread chapter sixteen on facing reality.
    - ▪ That is the response of a weak manager.

Players are different today than in previous generations. The money is unimaginable to the typical worker. Egos can get out of control. Free agency has led to the end of player, and team, loyalty. What hasn't changed? Good coaches may make subtle changes to deal with the times, but they are never willing to compromise their core commitment to excellence. Expectations and demands are made of every player, from the one making the minimum salary, to the player who just received the twenty-million-dollar bonus.

➤ Researching a large cross-section of articles dealing with the abuse of the Internet at the workplace, there are numerous estimates, but a reasonable figure would be that the average employee spends seventy-five minutes per day on the Internet on non-work-related issues.
  - o Use your expensive formal education and break that down financially:
    - ▪ If you have one hundred employees, that translates into employing at least fifteen people who are surplus. If the average package is $50,000, that represents $750,000 per year that your company is wasting, and management is responsible for moving those dollars to the bottom line.
      - • If you allow people to develop bad workplace habits, they will develop bad workplace habits, and management must accept the responsibility.

KEY – Be a professional

- Continuing with the example above, if you have one thousand employees, the wasted money would be $7,500,000!
    - How hard does your company have to work to move that kind of money to the bottom line?
  - Taking a positive perspective, consider how much potential productivity there is in your current organization that is just waiting to be unlocked!
    - An additional benefit, an essential benefit, is that the employees will realize that they are accountable for their time, which was addressed in chapter nine.
      - Place the bar where it belongs.

What would this level of distraction mean to the football team?

- *During practice, this would translate into taking nine minutes off by every player, every hour.*
  - *Best case, they are wasting time and money.*
  - *Worst case, they are wasting time, money, and allowing the competition, who is utilizing every minute of their practice time, to improve at a faster rate and create a competitive advantage.*
- *How about competing in games using the same assumptions:*
  - *On first and second down, the team sends only nine players out on the field.*
  - *On third down, things improve, and they play with ten players.*
  - *Another alternative would be to play all eleven players, but not bother to participate at all in the last nine minutes of every game.*

KEY – Does this make sense?

Would we consider a coach a genius if he committed to utilizing all eleven players on the field every down? We expect all of the players to be fully engaged on every play. It seems even an absurd topic for conversation.

- o Should you expect any less from the "players" within your own profession?
  - ▪ Why do we routinely accept so much less?
- ➢ I have heard it repeatedly said that if the company gets aggressive in this area, they might lose employees or damage morale.
  - o Let's get this straight; if you ask people to work while they are at work, they might get mad or quit.
    - ▪ Good. Those are the employees you need to leave your company. If people are upset about working while at work, you should be helping them to the door, not trying to accommodate their unacceptable work ethic.
      - • *__You will lose__* if you establish expectations that anyone can reach.

KEY – Never get too comfortable

O.C.:   *"Coach, our quarterback got really upset with me because I told him that he needed to take the snap on every play. I'm afraid that if I push the issue, he may try the free agency market after the season. The last thing I want to do is spend my summer trying to find a new quarterback."*

The only decision that the Head Coach must make in this situation is who goes first — the quarterback or the coach.

- ➢ Good employees are essential to any organization.
  - o If you choose not to deal with the ones who are unproductive:

- The good employees will eventually leave to join a high-performance company.
- Worse yet, they may begin to adapt to the underachieving attitude that such an environment will reinforce.
  - You will be left with an entire business full of employees who are underachievers, and comfortable with it.
- You cannot be afraid to part ways with employees who are "work adverse."
  - It's a short-term pain that you must accept in exchange for long-term success.

KEY – Be a professional

Putting speakers in the quarterback's helmet was a fundamental communications change at the professional level. Signals from the sideline could no longer be stolen by the defense or misinterpreted by the quarterback. Offensive Coordinators didn't have to worry about juggling in players from the sidelines to bring in plays; they could concentrate on getting the most appropriate players on the field for the formation called. Errors in communication were dramatically reduced, and valuable seconds were freed up for the quarterback to read the defensive formation before the snap.

The key to the success of this new tool was that communication was limited to a few seconds each down. Just because the quarterback suddenly had access to advanced communications didn't mean that he was provided with a remote control so that he could keep track of other games, or check in with his agent to make sure that he was getting his share of airtime. An external plug wasn't included so that he could fire up his favorite video game or check his email during time-outs. The tool is effective because throughout the game, during work time, it's utilized only when beneficial, and only in a manner that helps the entire team.

Chapter 18

Playing for Money
Managing the Top Line

I t really is very simple, assuming that you are not inflating short-term numbers by sacrificing the future, the larger the difference between revenue and cost, the better for the organization. At the most basic possible level, expanding this gap has three separate facets, of which two are normally the focal points of companies. Cost reduction programs have achieved cult-like status, with classes, seminars, speakers, and internal experts given battle-worthy titles such as "black belt" or "champion" to emphasize their importance throughout the organization. On the revenue side of the equation, the most dynamic individuals battle for assignments to new markets and product launches that increase the top line, and define careers. The third leg of our stool, the neglected leg, is current pricing. In almost every business it represents the fastest way to increase profits, but at the same time receives the least amount of attention. Silently, it offers tremendous upside, but if left unattended can develop into a silent company killer.

> ➢ Throughout the majority of organizations, once you have secured
> the business, maintaining pricing becomes relegated to the back
> burner.

- o It's just not a very sexy aspect of managing a business.
  - ▪ Most individuals in sales and marketing are more likely to describe it as a painful part of the job that they prefer to avoid.
- o While your company goes about pursuing the next piece of business or exploring new markets, the margins on current business are left to slowly erode one percentage point at a time, and frequently it's only noticed when it reaches the point of crisis.

KEY – Never get too comfortable

A new wrinkle in the offense, which was poorly executed late in the game, became the post-game focal point as analysts questioned their change in strategy. In the morning papers, surrendering a key first down late in the game was dissected and blamed on the coaching staff. Despite what the media was proclaiming, as the team sat reviewing the game film the following week, reality painfully revealed itself time and time again. Regardless of changes in the offensive and defensive schemes receiving all of the media attention, their failure to block and tackle effectively was obviously at the root of their problems, and if they didn't fix those deficiencies, the specifics of the game plan were irrelevant.

- ➢ If you don't stay on top of current pricing within your business, by the time you finally realize that you have a problem and approach the customer, it will remain painful, and you will now have the added benefit of looking stupid — because you were.
  - o To continue driving profitability, you must commit to maintaining margins on current business as a central aspect of the business.
- ➢ It's natural for an aggressive organization to constantly focus on:
  - o The next big project that dramatically increases sales or expands the company's product or customer base.

- o Cost reduction programs that are featured in the annual report.
  - ▪ Six-sigma, Kaizen, or the flavor of the week program.
- o Implementation of the next level of quality certification mandated by your largest customer.
- o The new computer system that every department has been meeting on for the last six months.
- ➤ Justifiably, there is a lot of time and effort concentrated in these areas of the business. However, current pricing, which offers the fastest economic improvement, becomes the ugly stepsister and gets very little attention. Why?
  - o Because trying to maximize pricing is never popular with the customer.

Flaw – Ask how hard something is

- o It's hard to get people excited about your one percent price increase.
  - ▪ That is except for those who truly understand the economics of such an accomplishment (you need to be one of those people).
    - • If your company makes ten percent at the bottom line, a one percent price increase represents a ten percent improvement in profits.
    - • If your company makes five percent at the bottom line, a one percent price increase represents a twenty percent improvement in profits.
      - o Everyone should get excited about that.
- ➤ It's an inescapable fact of business that you must focus on the pricing of all of your products and services at all steps throughout

their life cycle.
- o How to raise them.
- o How to maintain them.
  - In a competitive investment environment where constantly growing the profitability of your organization isn't just an objective, but more likely a mandate, allowing margins to erode on current products is not an option.
- o This can manifest itself both in terms of price increases and minimizing, or holding off, price reductions.
  - Reality check — the price is what the market is willing to pay for your product. Regardless of whether that is above or below your current price, your objective must always be to maximize that number.

KEY - Business 101

Consider the changes in the world of professional football. Both the fans in the stadium and the television audience have an exponentially expanding variety of ways to spend their finite entertainment time and dollars.

- *The NASCAR audience has grown rapidly.*
- *Professional golf has its own channel.*
- *Poker has suddenly become a national craze and seems to be on multiple channels every day.*
- *ESPN has added so many new programs that I can't even find most them.*

In addition to these obvious competitors, professional football is not just competing with rival sports programming; it is competing with any other options for the time and money of their customers.

- *Video games.*
- *iPods.*
- *Movies.*
- *The Internet.*
- *Concerts.*

These alternative choices represent the competition for their customers' attention, and they are growing more intense every day. To date, professional football has been able to remain the preferred choice of its customer base, expand its market position, and dramatically increase its top line.

➢ Elevating the awareness of the profitability of your current products or services is a critical aspect of the business that will force you to deal with your strengths and weaknesses.

KEY – Be a professional

○ If you are in a market where you have to maintain or even lower prices as your cost base goes up, you are not in a sustainable position and cannot wait to take action.
  - This focus on pricing cannot avoid exposing your market position and weakness. It demands that your organization deal with:
    - Do you have pricing power? If not,
      - How do you achieve pricing power?
      - Are you investing resources in areas where you can earn it?
      - What is different about your offering?
      - Do you have a cost advantage?
      - What new offerings are you developing?
  - These should not represent difficult questions to

answer. If they are, then you have failed to create pricing power, and you need to focus on obtaining it in as many segments of your business as possible.

Both the players and the league have established and maintained pricing power. They continue to offer a unique product and make it difficult for new competitors to enter the market. Players who can compete and win at the professional level are very difficult to find and develop. The players' product is their ability to play the game. As long as they can perform at the peak level, they can command salaries that are much higher than other professions due to the universal laws of supply and demand. Note that when their abilities begin to diminish through injuries or age, they lose their pricing power. The result is that they sign for the veteran minimum, or even find themselves out of the game.

The league has developed a very loyal market, and created an environment where the barriers of entry for potential competitors are both extremely expensive and very high risk. Ask those associated with the failed USFL and XFL how the risk/reward worked out for them. They are constantly working to expand their market beyond its traditional base. The European never drew large crowds; however, it worked to expose that market, which is larger than the U.S., to the sport. Games are now played in Mexico, a logical development that will open the market to our neighbor in the south. The television market continues to enlarge around the globe, offering years of potential expansion. The league is also constantly trying to improve its current product, from changes as simple as updating team uniforms, implementing instant replay, and safeguarding the players.

- *With these strong positions, both the players and the league have established pricing power with their respective customers, and they are not afraid to charge for their product!*

➤ You must fight for your price all of the time.
   o Your customers are battling to lower your price; why would you commit any less effort to maximizing them?

- There is constant pressure to lower pricing, and you must push back.
  o Simultaneously, you must create a legitimate reason to fight back.
➤ Your customer demanding a cost down is no great intellectual insight developed through years of study at our most prestigious universities.
  o It represents the simplest of all possible purchasing strategies.
  o They don't need to understand your company, the marketplace, the economy, technological advancements, or even go through the effort of identifying and qualifying new sources.
  o They just put out their hand and say "gimmie" as loud and often as possible, knowing that most companies don't actually know their market position, and will begin to blindly negotiate.
    - First, you must thoroughly understand your market position.
    - Then, relentlessly work to maximize your price.
➤ Regardless of whether you are in manufacturing, service, or a professional line of business, there will be constant pressure on your cost base.
  o Raw material increases.
  o Labor increases.
  o Health care increases.
  o Utility increases.
  o Rent increases.
    - If your cost basis is going up, you must find a way to raise your revenue line.
      • If you fail, it's a mathematical certainty that you will eventually go out of business.

KEY – Facts are stubborn things

- o Become obsessed with pushing back, pushing up, wherever possible.

The franchise is reviewing ticket and concession pricing for the upcoming season. Like any business, it needs to establish the pricing structure that maximizes revenue. This optimal price may actually result in a few empty seats. In the same way, if your company is getting every piece of potential business, you aren't charging enough.

- ➢ Pricing power is where smart investors look for company strength.
  - o It's something that you earn, and it is essential if you are going to avoid being at the mercy of your customers.
    - ▪ This must be a key part of any company's strategic plan. Long term, participating only in markets where you have something unique to offer.
  - o These are the tough issues that managers are paid to address.
    - ▪ Success in this area does not happen by accident.

KEY – Be a professional

Management is locked in a constant struggle to balance its needs with the salary cap. Players who are still capable of making a contribution are released because less expensive players with similar abilities become available. There are new licensing fees, team publications, and a few more luxury suites that can be squeezed in to raise revenue. Management even puts annual bids out for cleaning crews in an effort to control costs. These are all important parts of managing a franchise, but the team cannot neglect the potential of the sixty thousand fans in the stands for every home game. Five dollars each in any combination of ticket prices, parking, concessions, or souvenirs is an additional three hundred thousand dollars per game. With eight regular season, and two preseason, games per year, that amounts to three million extra dollars annually. Raise the target to an additional ten dollars per seat, and revenue is up six million dollars. While every owner is searching for the next great income stream, they cannot neglect the potential increased revenue available from their current product offerings.

Chapter 19

The Playbook
Tell Employees What They Need to Do

As has been covered, making and maintaining detailed strategic plans is essential to the sustained success of any business, but it represents only the beginning. Your plan must be constantly communicated throughout the organization, and adapted to the realities unfolding in the marketplace. Finally, every employee must understand their role in the plan and what is expected of them. The only way for them to know what is specifically required is for someone to tell them. All too often, the employee is left to guess, then criticized for not coming to the correct conclusion. With some employees, this direction can be general, but with others, it must be painfully detailed. Regardless of the depth required, the essential requirement remains the same; employees must be told what to do, and then be followed up on.

- Instructing employees on what to do oftentimes appears to be a lost art in modern management.
    - It's just not considered proper.
- "Progressive" managers (defined as those rarely responsible for profit) frown on providing specific direction as being a backward and outdated methodology.

- o We have become so concerned about hurting people's feelings, making sure that they are satisfied with their job, and accommodating them in a manner that keeps them happy, that management neglects their primary responsibility:
  - ▪ Ensuring that their job contributes to the value of the organization.

KEY - Business 101

- ➢ The alternative to the management discipline of instructing employees regarding expectations is the increasingly popular environment where everyone gets to decide what is best.
  - o Directing your business in this manner is a sociological experiment, rather than a responsible, scientific, professional approach.
    - ▪ Non-managers and poor managers almost always advocate this approach.
      - • It provides them with an excuse to avoid the hard issues.
      - • Besides, it just feels better.

Flaw – Management by fuzzy feeling

- ➢ Real management starts with the goals of the organization.
  - o They reach out and constantly solicit input and feedback from as many sources as possible, and then:
    - ▪ Makes decisions and gives appropriate guidance to meet company objectives.

KEY – Be a professional

How is the football team doing with this coaching approach? It's not enough to know that they want to win. Every team, every player, wants to win. It's not enough to know that the team is on offense. Granted, an improvement from simply knowing that they want to win the game, but which players are responsible for what assignments? It's not enough to know the starting lineup (i.e. the organizational chart). All eleven players on the field cannot run their own plays just because they were enlightened enough to know that they needed to be on the field. It's not enough to just call the play.

- *Are the right players on the field for the play?*
- *Do all of the players know the play?*
- *Do they know their assignments?*
- *Are they capable of performing their assignments?*

It's essential that someone is not only responsible for making the decision concerning which play is called, but takes the responsibility for ensuring that the players are in positions where they can succeed, and are properly trained to carry out their assignments. The players then execute the play utilizing their unique talents and experience, however, with specific, coordinated direction as part of the overall game plan.

➤ Ideally, management hasn't allowed an environment to be established where they must constantly instruct employees exactly how to accomplish every task, every day.
  o Nevertheless, it remains management's responsibility to direct and coordinate their employees' actions in a manner that moves the company forward, regardless of the level of involvement required.
    ▪ Although many modern managers refuse to acknowledge it, be prepared for the reality that far too many employees need to be told precisely what to do, how to do it, and when to do it.

KEY – Facts are stubborn things

➢ Despite some recent philosophies that all employees will take the initiative when given the opportunity, I have seen far too many people through too many years in too many situations who refuse to take any initiative to buy into such a sweeping assumption.

    o You have to be honest. Some employees just want to come to work, be told what to do, collect their paychecks, complain about management, and then go home.

        ▪ They prefer to go through life without taking any initiative.

            • Wishing that it were different isn't cause for following a flawed management philosophy.

    o Once you have provided direction, your work still isn't done.

        ▪ You must always follow up.

    o It's a noble, even essential habit to recognize employees for doing a good job. Part of management's responsibility is to provide positive reinforcement whenever possible, but remember the basic employment contract; it's a job, and they are paid to do it well.

        ▪ You are paying people to do a good job, not a marginal, sloppy, or uninspired job.

The middle linebacker makes a tackle four yards down field on first down and pumps his fist at the crowd and does a little dance step. In the grand scheme of the game, that may represent a marginally acceptable outcome, but not exactly time for celebrations and accolades. After all, making tackles is the linebacker's job. He's paid an exorbitant amount of money to make tackles. If anything, he should apologize to his teammates for not stopping the ball carrier two yards shorter. He needs to make the tackle and then get on with the next play without expecting cheers from the crowd. That is how professionals behave.

➢ A simple equation that our culture has chosen to ignore:

184

- o Work = pay.
  - If you don't like the pay of your current position and feel that you deserve more, get another job and demonstrate that you are worth more.
  - If you don't like the work and deserve better, find another job.
    - What is not acceptable is sitting around complaining about it day after day.
- o Employment is a business deal, hopefully, a deal where all parties involved feel satisfied with the terms, but that makes it no less a business deal.
  - Stop whining.
  - Make the most of yourself and your opportunities, and then go get the best deal you can.

Every player has unique talents and abilities. They are world-class athletes individually capable of far more than the average person on the football field. Nevertheless, every play is broken down into minute details to give the team the best opportunity for success. The linebacker with sprinter speed may have the ability to chase running backs down from sideline to sideline, but he is instructed that if he wants to play, he will maintain his containment discipline and remain committed to the responsibilities of the position. The players are allowed to use their considerable skills; however, with specific, detailed direction that benefits the entire team.

Chapter **20**

A Passion for Winning
Keeping Everyone Committed

I have always found that dealing with the human race is by far the most challenging, and all too often frustrating, part of managing a business. And although I have had a fair number of difficult customers to try to work with, it has always been employees that ultimately caused me the most grief. Even more aggravating, the pain always increased exponentially when I failed to deal with the problem person in a timely manner. It becomes a self-imposed misery created by non-action. Managing personnel issues is never easy; however, they must be dealt with. There is no easy way out, and theories that promise such invariably lead to even larger problems. Dealing with the tough issues sooner rather than later is the only way to keep the remainder of your workforce focused on their objectives.

> - It's a mistake to assume that everyone in the organization wants to do a good job. It's just too convenient of an all-encompassing philosophy to be realistic.
>   - o Yes, I realize that this is a politically incorrect management position.
>   - ▪ That doesn't negate the facts of life in the real world.

- In most circumstances, the vast majority of your company's employees will be committed to doing a good job.
  - Taking it a step further, this feel-good philosophy claims that if employees aren't doing a good job, it's always management's fault.
    - In some cases, this may be true; however, sometimes it actually is the fault of the employee.
      - You will note that the portrayers of this particular thought process deny any issues with their own employees.
        - That is if they have any. Many times those pushing this mantra are lone eagles because no one can stand working for them.
- The real-life philosophy should be that it is management's responsibility to give every employee the opportunity to do a good job.
  - It remains the employee's responsibility to take advantage of that opportunity.

The first few days of training camp are always riddled with errors and poor execution as the players readjust to the speed of the game. At the close of the first day, the General Manager and the Head Coach aren't worried about errors in execution; those are problems that they can correct over the next couple of weeks. What concerns them is the lack of conditioning apparent in the defensive back they selected in the second round of the draft the previous year.

G.M.:   *"After last season, we had a long talk with him about his lack of commitment, and against our advice, he insisted on doing all of his off-season training back with his college team."*

Head Coach: *"And here he is, twenty pounds overweight and a step too slow."*

G.M.: *"We have a lot invested in him. Can you bring him around?"*

Head Coach: *"He's not even in good enough condition to effectively participate in drills, and it's frustrating everyone around him after only one day. I'm meeting with him in a few minutes in my office to let him know that he's out of all drills and assigned to the trainers until he drops at least ten pounds. If he's not back to full speed by the second preseason game, he's gone."*

G.M.: *"Make sure that your position is clear."*

Head Coach: *"I will leave no doubt that my expectations are the same for him as any other player on this team. Roster spots aren't handed out, they're earned."*

- ➤ I have seen many managers latch onto the assumption that every employee will always take the initiative if just given the opportunity, as a "no exceptions" philosophy.
  - o My first thoughts are; have they actually ever managed people and been held accountable for their success?

Flaw – Management by fuzzy feeling

- o The only way for a manager to truly believe this is legitimate is to be completely out of touch with the real world.
  - ▪ Another feel-good management philosophy that ignores reality because it's easier.
- o Reality - some employees intentionally do as little as possible.
- o Reality - some employees unintentionally do as little as possible.

- Why is it so difficult to acknowledge the obvious?
  o Warning - you can never use this reality as an excuse to not expect that all employees want to do a good job.

KEY – Facts are stubborn things

- As small as it may be, there is a percentage of the human race that doesn't care, and never will care.
➢ Most managers have had to struggle with numerous underachieving employees. I once had to deal with an employee who insisted on telling the workers around her to slow down and not work so hard. Obviously, this created some friction within the work area, because the majority of the employees sincerely wanted to do a good job.
  o Calling this employee in to discuss the problem quickly revealed the fundamental problem:
    - It wasn't that management hadn't set clear objectives.
      • Everyone understood the expectations.
    - It wasn't that management had set unrealistic objectives.
      • The workers had been instrumental in setting the standards.
    - It wasn't a lack of training.
      • The other workers not only had proven capable, they met the standards on a consistent basis.
  o The problem was that the employee wanted to do the least amount possible. For all of our enlightened beliefs, it was no more complicated than she just didn't care.

Flaw – Lack of integrity

- Even slapped in the face with this reality, we still managed to make it worse, and kept her on board, allowing her to spread poison, which was my fault.
- ➤ How about a real objective:
  - o Insist on working with employees who honestly want to do a good job.

G.M.:   *"You keep a free agent from a division-three school and cut a number-two draft choice, and the press is going to have a lot of questions for us."*

Head Coach: *"If I keep a high draft choice who is chronically overweight, underachieving, and stands on the sideline every game instead of a rookie free agent who regularly makes big plays that help the team, and the players on this team will have a lot of questions."*

KEY – Be a professional

- ➤ Hippie management is not professional management.
  - o When it comes to personnel issues, there are no absolutes, and pretending that there are isn't just naïve, it's poor management.
  - o Hopefully, these uninterested employees will eventually mature into individuals with the self-motivation to make a contribution, but if we are totally honest, some people just never learn to care.
  - o Preaching a moral philosophy as an absolute is a cop-out taken by managers who are too lazy to deal with real issues.
    - It may be the management.
    - It may be the employee.

- Presupposing either position is always the answer is extremely weak management.

Flaw – Bad Management

- ➤ Do the job of a professional manager.
  - o Once you have established the goals and objectives for the organization:
    - ▪ Determine what is required to achieve those objectives.
      - Do you have the resources?
      - Identify areas of weakness and then develop a plan to address them.

KEY – Be a professional

- ▪ Establish standards for the individual positions based on what is required.
  - Do everything you can to help every individual succeed.
- ▪ Have enough faith in people to set expectations where they belong.
- ▪ Always treat everyone fairly, providing him or her the opportunity to succeed.
- ▪ Take the long view.
  - In the end, the person must be able ***and willing*** to do the job.
- o The new world will not allow employees to come to work and just collect a check.
- o The new world will not allow managers to adopt shallow philosophies that provide them with an excuse not to deal with difficult personnel issues.

Flaw – Management by fuzzy feeling

A player who shows up for training camp and goes through the motions, doing as little as they can get away with, will never survive at the professional level. Even if he has the talent, the competition is too fierce for him to excel. The team needs his best effort on every play, and that starts at the first practice. Secondly, the coaches cannot allow his attitude and work habits to permeate the team. The player with the least amount of commitment establishes the minimum standard for behavior. Finally, they cannot waste precious time trying to develop a player who isn't totally committed. The coaches have no choice but to provide the player the freedom to test the free agency market. Their job is to provide the opportunity for the player to be successful, but the player must actively take advantage of that opportunity.

SUMMARY
A New Season

S o, that's it, twenty brief chapters, five keys to success, five company-killing flaws, and a return to common sense. When you find yourself faced with what seems an insurmountable problem, revisit the keys and flaws, and take a few seconds to think, adjust, and then address the problem.

KEYS
1 - Business 101
2 - Be a professional
3 - Keep asking, Does this make sense?
4 - Never get too comfortable
5 - Facts are stubborn things

FLAWS
1 - Bad management
2 - Debating if change is good or bad
3 - Management by fuzzy feeling
4 - Lack of integrity
5 - Ask how hard something is

If you find yourself at a complete loss, put on your helmet and consider what the coach would do in a similar situation facing him on the football field. Leaders aren't always right, but they are always moving forward. If you make a mistake, admit it and press on. When the world suddenly changes around you, put your emotions aside, evaluate the threats and opportunities, and then start making decisions based on reality. Finally, at the risk of sounding fuzzy, take your career, not yourself, seriously, and remember to have some fun.

Printed in the United States
200074BV00007B/106-138/A

9 781432 708061